BOS COOKS

BALTIMORE OUTREACH SERVICES CULINARY ARTS

with Chef Connie Crabtree-Burritt

BOS CŒKS

BALTIMORE OUTREACH SERVICES CULINARY ARTS
with Chef Connie Crabtree-Burritt

Copyright © 2013 by
Baltimore Outreach Services
701 South Charles Street
Baltimore, Maryland 21230
410-752-7179

Cover illustration © by Crystal Moll
Back cover and food photography © by Steffi Graham
Original Art:
page 4 © by Bruno Baran; page 10 © by Stewart White; page 30 © by David Herman
page 60 © by Lisa Egeli; page 74 © by Hai-Ou Hou; page 114 © by Tim Kelly
page 152 © by Mark Cottman; page 170 © by Bill Wilson; page 186 © by David Herman

Manufactured and Produced by

Favorite Recipes® Press

An imprint of

SOUTHWESTERN
Publishing Group

P.O. Box 305142, Nashville, Tennessee 37230
1-800-358-0560

Art Direction and Book Design: Steve Newman
Recipe Editor: Nicki Pendleton Wood, CCP
Project Manager: Cathy Ropp

Library of Congress Control Number: 2012913348
ISBN: 978-0-615-62924-7

This cookbook is a collection of favorite recipes, which are not necessarily original recipes.

Manufactured in the United States of America
First Printing: 2013   5,000 copies

BOS COOKS

BALTIMORE OUTREACH SERVICES CULINARY ARTS
with Chef Connie Crabtree-Burritt

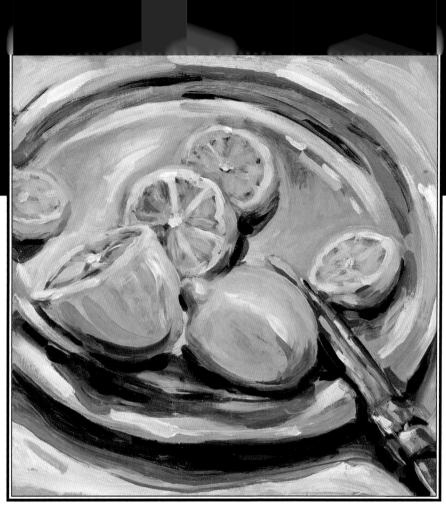

Bruno Baran

*BOS Cooks is dedicated to
homeless women and children, staff, and supporters
who share a journey of hope and hard work.*

Together we are successful.

BOS gratefully acknowledges the commitment and contributions to the culinary arts program by the organizations and individuals named below.

The Abell Foundation
Baltimore Women's Giving Circle
The Dresher Foundation
Emmanuel Episcopal Church
Les Dames d'Escoffier
Dawn Carlson
Pat & Jim Goodyear
Mary & Harold Graul
The Harry & Jeanette Weinberg Foundation
Anne & Christopher West

PROFESSIONAL CREDITS

FRONT COVER ARTIST

Crystal Moll

ARTISTS

Bruno Baran — Lemons illustration (page 4)
Stewart White — Appetizers & Hors d'Oeuvre
David Herman — Soups, Salads, & Sandwiches
Lisa Egeli — Vegetables & Sides
Hai-Ou Hou — Brunch & Breads
Tim Kelly — Main Dishes
Mark Cottman — Pasta & Grain
Bill Wilson — Condiments & Sauces
David Herman — Desserts

FOOD & BACK COVER PHOTOGRAPHY

Steffi Graham

Left to right in back cover photograph

Latitia Carter, Culinary Graduate; Connie Crabtree-Burritt, Chef;
Michele Grey, Culinary Graduate; Posie Spratley, Sous Chef

FOOD PHOTOGRAPHY LAY-OUT

Diana Samet

Executive Steering Committee

Cookbook Chair

Connie Crabtree-Burritt

Editors

Susan Bridges	Anne West	Cathy Wood-Rupert

Committee

Karen Adkins	Pat Goodyear	Jane Sabatelli
Susan Bridges	Betty Higman	Deanna Urner
Connie Crabtree-Burritt	Susan Landry	Anne West
Donna Rich		Cathy Wood-Rupert

Sales and Marketing Committee

Karen Adkins	Gregg Landry	Takirra Wakefield
Susan Bridges	Cassie Motz	Susan Walther
Connie Crabtree-Burritt	Rodrigo Neder	Richard Walther
Pat Goodyear	Donna Rich	Anne West
Steffi Graham	Tammy Turner	Cathy Wood-Rupert

Stewart White

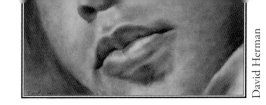
David Herman

APPETIZERS & HORS d'OEUVRE

SOUPS, SALADS & SANDWICHES

Lisa Egeli

Hai-Ou Hou

VEGETABLES & SIDE DISHES

BRUNCH & BREADS

Tim Kelly

Main Dishes
114

Mark Cottman

Pastas & Grains
152

Bill Wilson

Condiments & Sauces
170

David Herman

Desserts
186

APPETIZERS & HORS D'OEUVRE

Stewart White

"I never knew that people helped people they did not know until I came to this shelter. I am very grateful that BOS gave my family and I a place to live, food to eat, and clothes to wear. Then they helped me make a plan to get on my feet again."

Tairra

Former resident, living independently

The Beginning

In 1999 Baltimore City Government became alarmed with the number of women and children that were homeless. City representatives met with churches and community leaders to assess how to meet the needs of this vulnerable and growing population. At that time, Christ Lutheran Church was already providing emergency shelter in the undercroft of the church—paying utilities and providing daily meals.

Responding to the great community need, the Christ Church Council determined that serving homeless women and children would become a priority of the Church's mission. In 2002 Baltimore Outreach Services (BOS) was founded as an independent, nonprofit corporation. During the first years of operation, the financial resources were provided by the congregation of Christ Church, and day-to-day management was contracted through the YWCA of Maryland.

From the beginning, BOS has been committed to the core principle that in order to move from homelessness, residents need more than just emergency shelter. In 2005 BOS began direct management of the shelter, continuing to address the underlying causes of homelessness to promote long-term independence and self-sufficiency.

Menu

Sharp Cheese and Pecan Shortbread

Hot Maryland Crab Dip with Crostini

Bruschetta with Cannellini Bean and Olive Tapenade

Lettuce Wraps

Cocktail Meatballs with Strawberry Jalapeño Sauce

Almond Biscotti

Chocolate Cupcakes with Cream Cheese Frosting

When hosting an Hors d'Oeuvre Reception, one of the first considerations is how many different hors d'oeuvre and how many "bites" to offer. It is important to balance the menu with several choices and to have something for everyone. When the menu is intended to replace dinner and is being served all evening, eight or ten "bites" per guest should do it. Adding something sweet should bring the bite count up to a baker's dozen per guest. If dinner is being served, five or six bites is plenty.

ARTICHOKE NIBBLES

1 (14-ounce) can water-pack artichoke hearts
1 (6-ounce) jar marinated artichoke hearts
1 small onion, chopped
1 garlic clove, chopped
4 eggs
1/4 cup bread crumbs
1/4 teaspoon salt
1/2 teaspoon pepper
1/2 teaspoon oregano
1/2 teaspoon Tabasco sauce
8 ounces Cheddar cheese, shredded
2 tablespoons chopped parsley

Drain the water-pack artichokes and discard the liquid. Chop the artichokes. Drain the liquid from the marinated artichokes into a saucepan. Chop the artichokes. Add the onion and garlic to the artichoke marinade. Sauté for 5 minutes.

Beat the eggs in a bowl. Add the bread crumbs, salt, pepper, oregano and Tabasco sauce. Stir in the artichokes, onion mixture, cheese and parsley, mixing well. Pour into a 9×9-inch baking pan. Bake at 325 degrees for 30 minutes. Cut into squares.

Makes 9 servings

Jane Sabatelli

Tip: This dish can also be served as a side dish.

ALMOND-ENCRUSTED CHICKEN BITES WITH ZESTY DIPPING SAUCE

ZESTY DIPPING SAUCE
1 cup duck sauce
1/4 cup Tiger sauce
1 teaspoon Asian chili garlic sauce
1 tablespoon soy sauce

CHICKEN
2 boneless chicken breasts
Salt and pepper to taste
1/2 cup sliced almonds
1/2 cup cornflakes
1 cup panko (Japanese bread crumbs)
1 egg
1/2 cup milk
1 cup oil

For the sauce, combine the duck sauce, Tiger sauce, chili garlic sauce and soy sauce in a medium bowl and mix well.

For the chicken, cut each chicken breast into halves. Place the chicken between two sheets of waxed paper and pound to 1/2-inch thickness. Season on both sides with salt and pepper. Cut the chicken into bite-size pieces.

Pulse the almonds and cornflakes in a food processor several times to reduce them to rough crumbs. Add the panko and pulse several more times. Crumbs should be fine, but not powdery.

Beat the egg and milk together in a bowl. Dip each piece of chicken into the egg mixture. Coat with the panko mixture.

Heat the oil in a deep pan. Use a slotted spoon or tongs to lower several chicken pieces at a time into the hot oil. Cook for 5 minutes or until golden brown. Drain on paper towels. Keep warm. Serve with zesty dipping sauce.

Makes 6 servings

CRAB TARTLETS WITH CHILE-LIME SAUCE

TARTLET SHELLS
1 refrigerator pie pastry
1 tablespoon Dijon mustard

CHILE-LIME SAUCE AND ASSEMBLY
$1/2$ cup mayonnaise
$1/4$ cup sour cream
Zest and juice of 1 lime
1 tablespoon Tiger sauce
1 tablespoon capers, chopped, plus additional for garnish
$1/8$ teaspoon cayenne pepper
1 pound jumbo lump crab meat

For the tartlet shells, roll the pie pastry on a floured surface until it is thinner than normal pie pastry. Brush with the Dijon mustard. Cut into rounds with a 2-inch biscuit cutter. Press the rounds into lightly greased miniature muffin cups. Bake at 350 degrees for 15 minutes or until light brown. Cool and store in an airtight container until ready to use.

For the sauce and assembly, combine the mayonnaise, sour cream, lime zest, lime juice, Tiger sauce, 1 tablespoon capers and the cayenne pepper in a bowl and mix well.

Divide the crab meat among the tartlet shells. Top with the sauce. Garnish with chopped capers.

Makes 36 tartlets

FLATBREAD WITH GOAT CHEESE RICOTTA

FLATBREAD
6 to 7 cups all-purpose flour
1/2 tablespoon dry yeast
1/2 teaspoon salt
1 tablespoon dried thyme
1 tablespoon dried rosemary
3/4 cup plus 2 tablespoons olive oil
1 1/2 cups plus 1 tablespoon water

TOPPING
4 Roma tomatoes, chopped
1 1/4 cups goat cheese ricotta
1 garlic clove, minced
4 ounces sliced prosciutto
5 ounces baby arugula
1/4 cup olive oil
Salt and pepper to taste

For the flatbread, combine the flour, yeast, salt, thyme and rosemary in a mixer fitted with a dough hook. Add the olive oil and water and mix until the dough has a sticky consistency. Separate the dough into 5-ounce pieces (about 10). Cover with a clean kitchen towel. Let rise until doubled in size.

Punch down the dough balls. Shape into flat rounds and arrange on a baking sheet. Bake at 400 degrees for 7 to 8 minutes until golden brown.

For the topping, heat a cast-iron, steel or other noncoated skillet to very hot. Add the tomatoes to the pan and turn off the heat. Sear briefly, but do not overcook.

Combine the cheese and garlic and mix well. Drizzle the arugula with the olive oil. Season with salt and pepper.

Place a small amount of the cheese mixture on each flatbread. Top with the prosciutto, then the tomatoes. Arrange the arugula over the tomato.

Makes 8 to 10 servings

Chef Manolo Acin, The Harbor Court Hotel, Baltimore

Variations: If you can't find goat cheese ricotta, make your own using 30 percent goat cheese and 70 percent ricotta to create the full 10 ounces needed, or you can substitute 1/2 cup feta cheese for the goat cheese in the ricotta mixture.

NAAN WITH WALNUT PESTO AND FRESH MOZZARELLA

WALNUT PESTO
2 cups walnuts
1 cup fresh basil leaves
1 cup grated Parmesan cheese
2 cups olive oil

NAAN AND ASSEMBLY
1/2 tablespoon cornmeal
2 naan (East Indian flatbread)
3 cups cubed fresh mozzarella
1/2 cup kalamata olives, pitted and chopped

For the pesto, pulse the walnuts and basil in a blender or a food processor until roughly chopped. Add the cheese. Pour in the olive oil gradually with the motor running. Process until the mixture is smooth.

For the naan and assembly, sprinkle the cornmeal on a baking sheet. Spread 1/2 to 3/4 cup walnut pesto on each naan. Top with the cheese, then the olives. Bake at 400 degrees for 15 minutes or until the cheese is melted. Use a pizza wheel to cut into pieces. Serve warm.

Makes 6 servings

You don't have to cook fancy or complicated, just good food from fresh ingredients. —Julia Child

Cocktail Meatballs with Strawberry Jalapeño Sauce

Strawberry Jalapeño Sauce
1 (10-ounce) package frozen strawberries, thawed
2 cups barbecue sauce
1 cup ketchup
1/4 cup molasses
1 tablespoon Tiger sauce
1 teaspoon garlic pepper
1 jalapeño chile, seeded and chopped

Meatballs
1 1/2 pounds ground beef
1/4 cup minced onion
1 cup panko (Japanese bread crumbs)
1 large egg
1/4 cup milk
1/2 teaspoon garlic pepper
1/2 teaspoon chipotle chile powder
1/4 cup oil

For the sauce, purée the strawberries in a food processor or blender until smooth. Combine the barbecue sauce, ketchup, molasses, Tiger sauce and garlic pepper in a saucepan. Bring to a simmer over low heat. Add the puréed strawberries and cook until the mixture is thick. Stir in the jalapeño.

For the meatballs, combine the ground beef, onion, panko, egg, milk, garlic pepper and chile powder. Shape into miniature meatballs.

Brown the meatballs in the oil in a skillet over medium-high heat. Drain on paper towels. Set aside or refrigerate until ready to serve.

Combine the meatballs with the sauce in a saucepan. Heat until the meatballs reach an internal temperature of 165 degrees.

Makes 35 to 40 miniature meatballs

LOBSTER SPOONS

This recipe allows for a dramatic presentation while avoiding additional carbohydrates by placing the salad on decorative spoons rather than serving on crostini or crackers. The unique presentation is sure to make guests feel special without breaking the bank.

LOBSTER	SALAD
2 quarts (8 cups) water	1 orange, cut into sections
1 cup white wine	(see Tip below)
1 onion, cut into quarters	$1/2$ cup chopped pineapple
1 teaspoon black peppercorns	$1/2$ cup mayonnaise
3 bay leaves	Zest and juice of 1 lime
1 ($1^1/2$-pound) lobster	1 teaspoon chives, minced
	$1/4$ teaspoon cayenne pepper
	Dash of Tiger sauce
	Salt to taste

To cook the lobster, fill a large stockpot with the water. Add the wine, onion, peppercorns and bay leaves. Bring to a boil. Plunge the lobster in head first, then quickly cover the pot. Cook for 8 to 10 minutes. Remove the lobster from the liquid to cool. Crack the lobster shell and remove the meat. Slice into bite-size pieces.

For the salad, combine the orange and pineapple in a bowl. Add the mayonnaise, lime zest, lime juice, chives, cayenne pepper, Tiger sauce and salt and mix well. Fold in the lobster. Chill before serving.

Portion the lobster salad into flat-bottom Asian-style soup spoons and serve as an hors d'oeuvre.

Makes 6 servings

Tip: To section an orange, peel with a paring knife, being sure to remove the bitter white pith. Hold the orange over a bowl to catch the juices, and slice between the membranes and the sections of the orange. Lift the section out with the blade of the knife. Squeeze the juice from the remaining membrane of the orange.

SHRIMP AND CORN FRITTERS

1 1/4 cups white cornmeal
3/4 cup all-purpose flour
1 teaspoon sugar
1/2 teaspoon salt
1/2 teaspoon Old Bay seasoning
4 teaspoons baking powder
1 egg, beaten
1 cup milk
2 tablespoons butter, melted

1 tablespoon minced shallot
1 tablespoon chopped chives
Kernels from 2 ears of corn
8 ounces shrimp, peeled and
   coarsely chopped
Tabasco sauce to taste
1/2 cup (about) vegetable oil
Sour cream

Combine the cornmeal, flour, sugar, salt, Old Bay seasoning and baking powder in a bowl. Add the egg, milk, butter, shallot, chives, corn, shrimp and Tabasco sauce; mix well to form a thick batter that is not stiff.

Heat 1 tablespoon of the oil in a heavy skillet. Drop teaspoons of batter onto the skillet. Cook the fritters until brown on both sides, turning once. Drain on paper towels. Top each fritter with a dollop of sour cream.

Makes 36 fritters

Tip: *It's simple to cut corn from the cob. Set a wet paper towel*
on a cutting board. Slice off the bottom of the cob so the corn will
stand upright securely. Steady the cob with one hand at the top.
Use a sharp knife to slice kernels from top to bottom.

You only get one chance to make a good first impression. First impressions with food are also important. Appetizers and hors d'oeuvre set the tone for the rest of the meal. In class we talk about the impression we make when we meet someone and how important it is to be consistent and reliable. The same is true when working with food. I like relating a food lesson to a life lesson. After all, they both go a long way to sustain us. —The Chef

STUFFED BABY BELLA MUSHROOMS

1 pound bulk pork sausage
24 baby bella mushrooms
1/2 cup minced onion
1/4 cup (1 ounce) shredded Pepper
    Jack cheese
1 1/2 cups bread crumbs

1/2 cup (1 stick) butter, melted
1/4 cup fresh parsley, minced
1/4 teaspoon kosher salt
1/4 teaspoon pepper
1 3/4 cups (7 ounces) shredded
    Pepper Jack cheese

Brown the sausage in a skillet, stirring until crumbly; drain on paper towels. Drain all but 1 tablespoon of drippings from the skillet. Chop the mushroom stems; reserve the mushroom cups. Sauté with the onion in the reserved drippings.

Combine the sausage, onion mixture, 1/4 cup cheese, the bread crumbs, butter, parsley, salt and pepper and mix well. Spoon into the mushroom caps. Arrange on an ungreased baking sheet. Sprinkle with 1 3/4 cups cheese. Bake at 350 degrees for 25 minutes.

Makes 24 pieces

Betty Higman

SHARP CHEESE AND PECAN SHORTBREAD

2 cups all-purpose flour
1 cup (2 sticks) butter, softened
2 cups (8 ounces) finely shredded
    sharp Cheddar cheese
Cayenne pepper to taste

1/2 teaspoon kosher salt, or to taste
2 cups pecans, chopped
1 tablespoon chipotle chili powder
    (optional)

Pulse the flour, butter, cheese, cayenne pepper and salt in a food processor. Add the pecans and pulse a few times more.

Form the dough into two logs and wrap securely in waxed paper. Chill for about 1 hour. Cut the logs into rounds and arrange on a baking sheet. Press lightly with a fork to make an indentation. Sprinkle with the chili powder. Bake at 350 degrees for 10 minutes.

Makes 36 cookies

CANNELLINI BEAN AND OLIVE TAPENADE

1 (19-ounce) can
cannellini beans
2 cups pimento-stuffed
Spanish olives
1 (14-ounce) can petite-
diced tomatoes

1/4 cup chopped basil
1 tablespoon olive oil
1/4 teaspoon salt, or to taste
1/2 teaspoon freshly ground pepper
Crostini (page 91)

Drain the beans, olives and tomatoes. Pulse the beans in a food processor until roughly chopped. Spoon into a bowl. Repeat with the olives, then the tomatoes.

Add the basil, olive oil, salt and pepper to the bean mixture and mix lightly with a fork. Serve with Crostini.

Makes 8 to 10 servings

GUACAMOLE

4 large ripe avocados
1 large tomato, diced
1 small white onion, diced
Juice of 1 lime
2 or 3 small jalapeño chiles,
seeded and diced

2 tablespoons chopped fresh
cilantro, or to taste
1 teaspoon salt, or to taste
1 teaspoon pepper, or to taste

Peel and pit the avocados. Mash them in a bowl with a fork. Add the tomato, onion, lime juice and jalapeños and mix well. Season with the cilantro, salt and pepper.

Makes 10 servings

Lesley Miller

*Tip: To prevent guacamole from turning brown, try burying
the avocado pit in the center of the finished dip until ready to serve.*

CHOPPED LIVER

1 (7-ounce) package frozen
schmaltz (chicken fat), thawed
1 large onion, chopped
1 pound chicken livers

2 eggs, hard-cooked
Dash of Worcestershire sauce
Salt and pepper to taste

Heat half the schmaltz in a saucepan. Add the onion and sauté until translucent. Add the remaining schmaltz and the chicken livers and cook, taking care not to overcook the livers. Chill. Place the liver mixture, onions and eggs in a food processor. Pulse a few times. Spoon into a bowl and stir in the Worcestershire sauce, salt and pepper. Refrigerate until ready to serve. Serve as a spread with assorted crackers and flatbread.

Makes 10 to 12 servings

Marlene Meyer

Tip: Empire brand frozen schmaltz can be purchased in grocery stores, typically in the Jewish food section. If you cannot find schmaltz, substitute 1/2 cup (1 stick) of butter.

FOUR-CHEESE PIMENTO SPREAD

1 (4-ounce) jar diced
pimentos, drained
2 teaspoons sweet pickle juice
12 ounces white Cheddar
cheese, shredded
4 ounces Parmesan cheese, shredded

8 ounces yellow Cheddar
cheese, shredded
4 ounces feta or Gorgonzola
cheese, crumbled
3 tablespoons Dijon mustard
1 cup mayonnaise

Combine the pimentos, pickle juice, cheeses, Dijon mustard and mayonnaise in a large bowl. Chill, if desired. Serve with crackers or as a sandwich spread.

Makes about 2 1/2 pounds

Betty Robinson

Cheese: milk's leap toward immortality —Clifton Fadiman

23

REUBEN DIP

8 ounces cream cheese, softened
1/2 cup sour cream
2 tablespoons mayonnaise
1 cup sauerkraut, drained, rinsed
and chopped

8 ounces cooked corned beef,
chopped
2 tablespoons finely chopped onion
1 tablespoon spicy brown mustard
1 cup (4 ounces) shredded Swiss cheese

Combine the cream cheese, sour cream and mayonnaise in a bowl and mix well. Add the sauerkraut, corned beef, onion, mustard and cheese and mix well. Spoon into a lightly greased baking dish. Bake at 350 degrees for 30 minutes or until brown and bubbly. Serve hot with rye crackers or cocktail rye bread.

Makes 10 to 12 servings

Deanna Urner

FRESH SALSA

12 small vine-ripe tomatoes
3 or 4 small jalapeño chiles
1 white onion

Fresh cilantro to taste
Lime juice to taste
Salt to taste

Seed the tomatoes and jalapeños. (Or, for hot salsa, use the jalapeño seeds.)
Purée the tomatoes, jalapeños and onion in a large blender, working in batches if needed. Add cilantro, lime juice and salt and mix well.
Refrigerate the salsa, which will look frothy. Chilling allows the flavors to marry and restores the bright red color to the tomatoes.

Makes 12 servings

Lesley Miller

Tip: When working with chiles, it is recommended that you wear latex gloves. The natural oils from the chiles can stay on your skin and cause irritation. Also remember to keep your hands away from your eyes when working with chiles!

HOT MARYLAND CRAB DIP

24 ounces cream cheese
1/2 cup mayonnaise
1 tablespoon Dijon mustard
Juice of 1 lemon
1 teaspoon Worcestershire sauce
1/2 teaspoon Tabasco sauce
2 teaspoons Old Bay seasoning, or to taste
1 pound back-fin crab meat

Heat the cream cheese in a glass bowl in the microwave for 1 minute to soften. Add the mayonnaise, Dijon mustard, lemon juice, Worcestershire sauce, Tabasco sauce and Old Bay seasoning and mix well.

Check the crab meat for shells. Fold the crab meat into the cream cheese mixture, taking care not to break up the crab. The dip is best when the crab is still in large lumps.

Spoon the dip into a 9×9 ovenproof serving dish. Bake at 350 degrees for 25 to 30 minutes until light brown and bubbly. Serve with Crostini (page 91), pita chips or crackers.

Makes 12 to 15 servings

Tip: To keep the dip hot for an extended period, use a chafing dish. For an updated look, place a flat garden slate on a riser and heat with sterno. Set the hot serving dish on the slate.

SAVORY CHEESECAKE WITH POLENTA CRUST

CUSTARD
2 cups ricotta cheese
4 eggs, beaten
1 cup heavy cream
1 cup (4 ounces) grated
Parmesan cheese
$1/2$ cup (2 ounces) shredded
mozzarella
$1^1/2$ teaspoons salt
$1/2$ teaspoon cayenne pepper
1 teaspoon Italian seasoning

VEGETABLES
2 cups shredded zucchini
1 tablespoon olive oil
$1/2$ teaspoon salt
$1/2$ teaspoon pepper
1 cup (4 ounces) shredded mozzarella

POLENTA CRUST AND ASSEMBLY
1 shallot, minced
1 teaspoon salt
$1/4$ teaspoon cayenne pepper
1 tablespoon butter
3 cups chicken stock
$1^1/4$ cups dry polenta

For the custard, combine all the ingredients in a bowl and mix well. Set aside.

For the vegetables, sauté the zucchini in the olive oil in a skillet until tender. Add the salt and pepper. Drain the zucchini in a strainer over a bowl. Let cool. Combine the zucchini and mozzarella in a bowl and mix well. Set aside.

For the crust and assembly, sauté the shallot, salt and cayenne pepper in the butter in a sauté pan until the shallot is tender. Add the stock. Bring to a boil, then reduce the heat. Whisk in the polenta gradually. Remove the polenta from the heat when it begins to thicken. Pour into a springform pan, spreading it evenly over the bottom.

Spread the vegetables over the warm polenta; the cheese will begin to melt, which helps bind the layers. Pour the custard over the vegetables. Bake at 350 degrees for 40 to 50 minutes until the custard is set and light brown. Cool in the pan for at least 1 hour. Run a thin, sharp knife around the edge to loosen the cake, then remove the side.

Makes 8 to 10 servings

Variations: Cheesecake as an appetizer will surprise and delight your guests. Serve it with Marinara Sauce (page 185) or Cream Cheese Sauce (page 183) with $1/2$ cup gorgonzola added. The cheesecake also works as a luncheon entrée or first course.

EGGPLANT NAPOLEON

2 eggplant, each sliced into 8 rounds
1/2 cup lemon juice
1/2 cup milk
2 eggs
3 cups panko (Japanese bread crumbs)
1 teaspoon salt
1 teaspoon white pepper
1 tablespoon Italian seasoning
2 tablespoons olive oil
2 tomatoes, each sliced into 8 rounds
2 (8-ounce) balls fresh mozzarella, each sliced into 8 rounds
1/2 cup Walnut Pesto (page 178)
2 tablespoons pine nuts, toasted

Soak the eggplant slices with the lemon juice and water to cover in a bowl for 5 minutes. Lay the eggplant on paper towels and pat dry.

Combine the milk and eggs in a shallow bowl and mix well. Combine the bread crumbs, salt, white pepper and Italian seasoning in another shallow bowl. Dip the eggplant into the egg mixture then coat with the bread crumbs.

Heat the olive oil in a medium sauté pan. Brown the eggplant slices in the oil. Drain on paper towels. Keep warm in a 200-degree oven.

Stack the eggplant and mozzarella slices. Top each with a tomato slice. Drizzle with the Walnut Pesto. Sprinkle each serving with a few of the pine nuts.

Makes 16 servings

CAVIAR CREAM CHEESE PIE

12 ounces cream cheese, softened
2 tablespoons mayonnaise
1 tablespoon grated onion
1 teaspoon Worcestershire sauce
 (optional)
Zest of 1 lemon
2 tablespoons lemon juice

3 drops of Tabasco sauce, or to taste
3 tablespoons minced fresh parsley
1 (3- to 4-ounce) jar lumpfish
 caviar, drained
1/2 cup minced green onions
2 hard-cooked eggs, sliced into rounds
Paprika to taste

Combine the cream cheese and mayonnaise in a bowl. Beat with a fork or wooden spoon until smooth. Stir in the onion, Worcestershire sauce, half the lemon zest, the lemon juice, Tabasco sauce and parsley. Spoon into a serving bowl. Spread the cream cheese mixture up the side of the bowl to about 1 inch from the rim to create a "shell" in the bowl. Spread the caviar evenly over the cream cheese mixture. Sprinkle with the green onions. Arrange the eggs over the top. Garnish with the remaining lemon zest. Serve with crackers or Melba toast.

Makes 6 to 8 servings

Frieda Ulman

PESTO AND SPINACH TORTE

16 ounces cream cheese
8 ounces ricotta cheese
1/2 cup (2 ounces) grated
 Parmesan cheese
1/4 teaspoon salt
1/8 teaspoon cayenne pepper

3 eggs
1/4 cup Walnut Pesto (page 178)
1/4 cup Spinach Pesto (page 177)
1/4 cup bread crumbs
1/4 cup (1 ounce) grated
 Parmesan cheese

Beat the cream cheese, ricotta cheese, 1/2 cup Parmesan cheese, the salt and cayenne pepper until well blended. Add the eggs one at a time, beating well after each addition. Divide between two bowls. Stir the Walnut Pesto into one bowl and the Spinach Pesto into the other bowl. Combine the bread crumbs and 1/4 cup Parmesan cheese. Coat a buttered springform pan with the crumb mixture. Spread the spinach mixture in the pan. Top with the basil mixture. Bake at 325 degrees for 45 minutes. Let cool. Chill, covered, until serving time. Remove the side of the pan and serve with flatbread and crackers.

Makes 8 to 10 servings

LETTUCE WRAPS

CHICKEN FILLING

3 pounds boneless skinless
    chicken breasts
1 onion, diced
Zest of 1 lemon
Juice of 3 lemons
2 jalapeño chiles, seeded
    and minced
1 (9-ounce) jar chutney,
    large pieces diced
3 ribs celery, diced
1/2 cup mayonnaise
Salt and pepper to taste

WRAPS AND ASSEMBLY

1 head Bibb lettuce, leaves
    separated
Leaves from 1 bunch basil
Leaves from 1 bunch cilantro
8 large radishes, thinly sliced
1 large cucumber, peeled, seeded
    and sliced into rounds
1 cup salted almonds or
    cashews, chopped

For the filling, pour enough water into a large sauté pan to reach halfway up the side. Bring the water to a simmer. Add the chicken and simmer for 10 to 15 minutes until the chicken reaches an internal temperature of 165 degrees, turning once.

Cut the chicken into bite-size pieces. Combine with the onion, lemon zest, lemon juice, jalapeños, chutney, celery, mayonnaise, salt and pepper in a bowl and mix well.

For the wraps, arrange the lettuce leaves, basil, cilantro, radishes and cucumber around the perimeter of a serving platter. Spoon the chicken filling in the center. Sprinkle with the almonds.

Let each guest spoon chicken filling into a lettuce leaf and add their toppings of choice.

Makes 6 to 8 servings

Gail Shawe

*Tip: Lettuce wraps can be served as a salad or
for a light lunch. They often promote wonderful conversation
with friends and family.*

David Herman

"*The culinary training program is actually one of the best things that ever happened to me...I had been unemployable for years. I needed to be educated—not only in job skills, but life skills, which I never realized until I started the program. I learned how to dress, how to be on time, how to get up in the morning . . . I became a productive member of society again. Now I work 40 hours per week. I have health insurance. I have paid vacation. I have a 401(k) — these are things I never had in my life! It's been unbelievable for me.*"

Ella

Culinary graduate

The mission of Baltimore Outreach Services is to provide comprehensive services and programs to homeless women and their children. These services include emergency shelter, transitional housing, educational programming, health and mental health services, job training, and employment counseling.

Every night our residents gather together around a large table for meals and to share their struggles, triumphs, hopes, and happenings of the day. In much the same way, BOS gathers and provides for women in need around a larger "table" from which they can take the physical, emotional, educational, and therapeutic sustenance they need. This enables them to get back on their feet, learn new skills, and develop the capabilities and confidence they need to re-enter the larger community and sustain their own families.

Over the past decade many staff, donors, and volunteers have felt called to help this vulnerable population of women and children who simply do not have family and friends who can help them. For some of us, it has been a spiritual calling to serve the poor. For others, this is a women's issue. For all of us, our lives have been changed as we helped others to have the basics they need in the short term and the tools they need to empower and change their lives. In this process, we are all transformed.

CASUAL SUPPER WITH FRIENDS

Menu

Guacamole and Fresh Salsa
served with assorted tortilla chips

❖

Black Bean Soup

❖

Quesadillas with Pulled Pork and Chipotle Sweet Potatoes

❖

Shrimp Salad with Citrus Dressing

❖

Cheesecake Squares

❖

Oatmeal Chocolate Chip Cookies

This is a fun menu to serve at a casual gathering, especially if you have friends with hearty appetites. Everything on the menu can be prepared ahead and served buffet style. Try using mugs for soup rather than bowls.

MARYLAND CRAB SOUP

4 cups water	1 1/2 cups diced peeled potatoes
1 cup diced carrots	1 (14-ounce) can diced tomatoes
1 cup chopped onion	2 teaspoons parsley, chopped
1 1/4 cups chopped celery	1 tablespoon all-purpose flour
1/2 cup (1 stick) butter	1 cup water
1 teaspoon Old Bay seasoning	1 pound crab meat
1 teaspoon Worcestershire sauce	Salt and pepper to taste

Bring 4 cups water to a boil in a soup pot. Add the carrots, onion, celery, butter, Old Bay seasoning, Worcestershire sauce, potatoes, tomatoes and parsley. Reduce the heat and simmer for 1 hour. Whisk the flour into 1 cup water in a small bowl; stir into the soup. Cook until the soup has thickened, stirring constantly. Add the crab meat and cook until heated through. Season with salt and pepper.

Makes 6 to 8 servings

Bruce Kirby

CREAM OF CRAB SOUP

1 cup finely chopped onion	2 cups (about) half-and-half
1/4 teaspoon minced garlic	1 pound lump crab meat
1/4 cup (1/2 stick) butter	Sherry (optional)
2 tablespoons all-purpose flour	Old Bay seasoning to taste
4 cups chicken stock	Salt and pepper to taste
8 ounces cream cheese	

Sauté the onion and garlic in the butter in a large saucepan over medium heat until the onion is translucent. Add the flour and stir until no lumps remain. Add the stock gradually, whisking constantly. Add the cream cheese and heat until melted, stirring to mix well. Add 1 cup of the half-and-half. Cook until the soup thickens slightly, stirring frequently. Add additional half-and-half as needed if the soup seems too thick.

Add the crab meat and simmer for 5 minutes until heated through. Serve in warmed bowls; season servings with sherry, Old Bay seasoning, salt and pepper.

Makes 6 to 8 servings

CRÈME BALTIMORE

2 sweet potatoes, peeled and diced
2 white potatoes, peeled and diced
1 onion, diced
4 cups chicken stock
1 to 2 cups heavy cream
1/2 teaspoon curry powder
1 teaspoon Old Bay seasoning, or to taste
Salt and white pepper to taste
1 pound jumbo lump blue crab meat

Combine the sweet potatoes, white potatoes, onion and stock in a large saucepan and bring to a boil. Reduce the heat and simmer until the potatoes are very tender. Remove from the heat. Let cool.

Purée the cooled potato mixture in batches in a blender or food processor. Add 1 cup of the cream and the curry powder. Pour the soup through a strainer to remove any lumps or sweet potato fibers.

Chill the soup for several hours. Add more cream if the soup seems too thick. Season with the Old Bay seasoning, salt and white pepper. Serve chilled, garnishing each serving with the crab meat.

Makes 8 to 10 servings

Most students come into culinary job training with a limited résumé of foods they like to cook or eat. I like to start the students' culinary journey with our version of vichysoisse, a traditional chilled potato soup reinterpreted as a lightly curried sweet potato soup with a garnish of jumbo lump crab meat. In one bowl of soup, we learn a little French (vichysoisse), a little about spices of the Far East (Indian curry), and the elegance of Maryland's blue crab. Exposing students to unique flavors and new foods can open their minds to the importance of creativity and imagination in cooking. —The Chef

OYSTER STEW

^{1}/2 cup minced onion
^{1}/2 cup minced celery
1 cup diced red skin potatoes
1 garlic clove, minced
1 tablespoon butter
4 ounces cream cheese
^{1}/2 cup chicken stock
^{3}/4 cup milk
1 teaspoon Old Bay seasoning
^{1}/8 teaspoon cayenne pepper
^{1}/4 teaspoon white pepper
1 quart oysters with liquor
^{3}/4 cup heavy cream

Sauté the onion, celery, potatoes and garlic in the butter in a stockpot over medium heat until the vegetables are tender. Add the cream cheese and cook until it begins to melt. Add the stock, milk, Old Bay seasoning, cayenne pepper and white pepper. Reduce the heat and simmer until the vegetables are cooked through.

Add the oysters with liquor and the cream. Cook until the edges of the oysters begin to curl and are firm, but take care not to overcook the oysters. They should be tender, not chewy. Serve immediately.

Makes 6 to 8 servings

Tip: *Any stew, soup, or gravy can be thickened by adding a small amount of instant mashed potatoes. For the best results, stir in 1 teaspoon at a time until the desired thickness is reached.*

BOS Chili Cookoff Award Winner

*This recipe was entered into Metropolitan Café's Chili Cookoff
to benefit BOS. It was the people's choice and voted Number One!
"Next to music there is nothing that lifts the spirits and strengthens the
soul more than a good bowl of chili."*

3 pounds beef chuck,
cut in bite-size cubes
3 tablespoons vegetable oil
1 pound ground beef
2 cups diced red onions
$^1/2$ cup diced roasted
poblano chiles
$^1/2$ cup diced green bell pepper
3 garlic cloves, minced
3 beef bouillon cubes
1 cup tomato sauce
1 (6-ounce) can tomato paste
1 (28-ounce) can tomatoes
2 cups beef broth

1 (12-ounce) bottle beer
1 (14-ounce) can kidney beans
1 (10-ounce) can black-eyed peas
$^1/4$ teaspoon Tabasco sauce
2 tablespoons onion powder
$^1/4$ teaspoon cayenne pepper
1 teaspoon ground cumin
$^1/2$ teaspoon black pepper
5 tablespoons chili powder,
or to taste
2 teaspoons baking cocoa
$1^1/2$ tablespoons peanut butter
$^1/4$ teaspoon cinnamon, or to taste

Brown the chuck in 2 tablespoons of the oil in a large, heavy Dutch oven over medium-high heat. Remove the beef with a slotted spoon. Heat the remaining 1 tablespoon oil in the Dutch oven. Add the ground beef and cook until brown and crumbly. Add the onions, poblano chiles, bell pepper and garlic. Cook until the vegetables are tender.

Reduce the heat and add beef, bouillon cubes, tomato sauce, tomato paste, tomatoes, broth, beer, beans and black-eyed peas. Stir in the Tabasco sauce, onion powder, cayenne pepper, cumin, black pepper, chili powder, baking cocoa, peanut butter and cinnamon. Simmer for 2 hours, stirring often. The flavor is enhanced when the chili is prepared a day before serving.

Makes 10 to 12 servings

Aaron Fries

*This recipe contains a "secret ingredient"—peanut butter.
When using secret ingredients that are potential allergens, such as
nuts, be sure to inform guests before serving.*

WHITE TURKEY CHILI

This chili was also entered in the Chili Cookoff at Metropolitan Café. The cookoff raised funds for BOS, and most of the entrants were fiery hot red chilis. This white chili is a winner in its own right.

1 large onion, diced
1 tablespoon minced garlic
1/4 cup vegetable oil
1 1/2 pounds ground turkey
1 pound turkey breast meat, cubed
1 teaspoon ground cumin
1 teaspoon marjoram
1 bay leaf
4 cups chicken stock
1/2 teaspoon kosher salt, or to taste
1 cup pearl barley
1 (15-ounce) can chick-peas, drained and rinsed
1 small jalapeño chile, minced
1 cup (4 ounces) grated Cheddar cheese
1/2 cup chopped green onions

Sauté the onion and garlic in the oil in a stockpot until the onion is translucent. Add the ground turkey and cubed turkey. Sauté until brown. Add the cumin, marjoram and bay leaf and continue cooking. Add the stock and salt. Bring to a boil. Add the barley, chick-peas and jalapeño. Return to a boil. Reduce the heat and simmer for 45 minutes. Discard the bay leaf. Season with salt. Top with the cheese and green onions to serve.

Makes 6 to 8 servings

Betty Robinson

MINESTRONE

1 cup diced onion
2 garlic cloves, minced
1/2 cup diced celery
1/2 cup diced carrots
1 cup diced green beans
1 tablespoon olive oil
2 cups cubed ham
2 (14-ounce) cans diced tomatoes
1 (14-ounce) can cannellini beans, drained
4 cups chicken broth
1 tablespoon chopped basil
1 teaspoon Italian seasoning
1/2 teaspoon salt
1 teaspoon pepper
1 cup uncooked macaroni

Sauté the onion, garlic, celery, carrots and green beans in the olive oil in a stockpot until they begin to soften. Add the ham, tomatoes, beans, broth, basil, Italian seasoning, salt and pepper. Bring to a boil. Reduce the heat and simmer until the vegetables are tender. Add the macaroni and cook for 12 to 15 minutes until tender.

Makes 8 to 10 servings

It's a comforting thing to have, said Christopher Robin.
—A. A. Milne

BLACK BEAN SOUP

1 pound dried black beans
1 onion, diced
1 cup diced carrots
1 cup diced celery
3 garlic cloves, minced
2 tablespoons olive oil
1 (14-ounce) can
fire-roasted tomatoes
1 (10-ounce) can tomatoes and
green chiles
1 (6-ounce) can tomato paste
2 cups vegetable juice cocktail

4 cups beef stock
1 ham hock
Zest and juice of 1 lime
1 teaspoon chipotle chili powder
1 teaspoon thyme
1 ounce semisweet chocolate,
chopped
1 teaspoon salt
1 teaspoon pepper
Sliced avocado
Shredded white cheese
1 small red onion, chopped

Rinse and sort the beans. Cover with water in a pan. Soak for several hours or overnight.

Sauté the onion, carrots, celery and garlic in the olive oil in a stockpot until tender. Add the beans and soaking liquid. Add the tomatoes, tomato paste, vegetable juice cocktail, stock and ham hock. Bring to a boil, stirring frequently. Reduce the heat. Simmer for 2 hours or until the beans are tender. Add the lime zest, lime juice, chili powder, thyme, chocolate, salt and pepper. Remove from the heat to begin cooling. Purée half the soup in batches in a food processor. Return the puréed soup to the pot and simmer 1 hour longer, stirring frequently. Top with avocado, cheese and onion to serve.

Makes 8 to 10 servings

*Tips: This soup is not difficult, but it takes time.
It's important to stir and regulate the heat so the soup does
not burn. It tastes better the second day.
When cooking dried beans, salt should be added late in the
cooking process or it can toughen the bean skins.*

YELLOW LENTIL SOUP

2 pounds dried yellow lentils
2 white onions, diced
4 carrots, peeled and diced
2 turnips, peeled and diced
2 tablespoons olive oil
3 garlic cloves, minced
3 Roma tomatoes, seeded and diced
2 Yukon Gold potatoes, diced
Salt to taste
2 tablespoons olive oil
1 tablespoon McCormick ras el hanout, ground (see Tip below)
Pepper to taste
1/2 cup chopped parsley
Olive oil for drizzling

Rinse the lentils under running water until the water runs clear. Sauté half the onions, half the carrots and half the turnips in 2 tablespoons olive oil in a stockpot. Add the garlic, tomatoes, potatoes and salt. Add the lentils and enough water to cover by 2 inches. Simmer, covered, for 30 minutes, skimming any foam that forms on the surface.

Remove from the heat to cool slightly. Purée in a food processor until smooth. Sauté the remaining onion, carrots and turnips in 2 tablespoons olive oil. Add the ras el hanout and mix well. Add the lentil purée. Simmer until the soup thickens. If it becomes too thick, add water until soup is of the desired consistency.

Season with salt and pepper. Garnish servings with the parsley and drizzle with olive oil.

Makes 10 servings

Executive Chef Josean Rasado, Harbor Court Hotel

Tip: Ras el hanout is a popular Moroccan blend of spices that is used across North Africa. Although there is no set combination of spices, typically ras el hanout includes cardamom, cloves, cinnamon, ground dried chiles, coriander, cumin, nutmeg, peppercorns, and turmeric.

SPLIT PEA SOUP WITH CHAMPAGNE

1 pound split peas, rinsed
1 cup diced onion
1 cup diced celery
1 cup diced carrots
1 cup diced pancetta
2 garlic cloves, minced
1 tablespoon olive oil

1 teaspoon fresh thyme leaves
1/2 teaspoon cayenne pepper
6 cups chicken stock
Crème Fraîche (page 182)
Champagne
Crispy Shallots (recipe below)

Soak the peas in 1 quart water in a bowl for about 1 hour. Sauté the onion, celery, carrots, pancetta and garlic in the olive oil in a stockpot until the vegetables are tender. Add the thyme, cayenne pepper and peas with the soaking liquid. Add the stock and bring to a boil. Cover and reduce the heat to low. Cook for 2 hours or until the soup is thickened and the peas are tender, stirring frequently to prevent scorching.

Top each serving of soup with a dollop of crème fraîche, a splash of champagne and some Crispy Shallots.

CRISPY SHALLOTS

1/4 cup all-purpose flour
1/2 teaspoon salt
1/2 teaspoon pepper

6 shallots, thinly sliced
2 cups canola oil

Combine the flour, salt and pepper in a medium bowl. Separate the shallots into rings. Toss the shallots with the flour to lightly coat.

Fry a few shallot rings at a time in the hot oil in a saucepan. Drain on paper towels. Keep warm until ready to serve.

Makes 8 servings

*Tip: Chicken broth can be high in sodium, so be sure
to taste the soup before adding salt.*

CREAM OF BROCCOLI SOUP

2 cups broccoli florets, roughly chopped
1 cup broccoli stems, trimmed and finely chopped
1 cup chopped white onion
1 tablespoon olive oil
3 cups chicken stock
8 ounces cream cheese
4 ounces Velveeta cheese
1/2 teaspoon salt
1/2 teaspoon white pepper
1 pint (2 cups) heavy cream
1/4 cup (1 ounce) grated Parmesan cheese

Blanch the broccoli florets in boiling water in a saucepan for 1 minute. Plunge immediately into ice water to stop the cooking process; drain. Sauté the broccoli stems and onion in the olive oil in a large saucepan until the onions are translucent. Add the broccoli florets, stock, cream cheese, Velveeta, salt and white pepper. Reduce the heat and simmer for 15 minutes or until the florets are tender. Add the heavy cream and simmer for 15 minutes, stirring often so the soup does not scorch. Stir in the Parmesan cheese before serving.

Makes 4 to 6 servings

Tip: *An excellent use for leftover mashed potatoes is to add about 1/2 cup to cream soups as a thickener. Pre-portion amounts in freezer-safe sealable bags and freeze until needed.*

BUTTERNUT SQUASH SOUP

3 pounds butternut squash
2 cups chopped leeks,
white part only
1/2 cup chopped carrots
1/2 cup chopped celery
2 Granny Smith apples, peeled,
cored and chopped

1 tablespoon vegetable oil
Pinch of thyme
Pinch of sage
1/2 teaspoon white pepper
2 quarts (8 cups) chicken stock
Spiced Nuts (recipe below)

Cut the squash into halves and scoop out the seeds. Place cut side down on a baking sheet. Roast at 350 degrees for 45 minutes or until tender. Let cool. Scoop the squash from the shell.

Sauté the leeks, carrots, celery and apples in the oil in a Dutch oven until caramelized. Add the thyme, sage and white pepper. Add the squash and stock. Cook for 20 to 30 minutes. Remove from the heat and cool slightly. Purée the soup in a blender or food processor. Return to the Dutch oven and cook until heated through. Top each serving with Spiced Nuts.

SPICED NUTS

1/4 cup pecans, toasted
1/4 cup salted cashews
1 egg white

1/4 tablespoon cinnamon
1 tablespoon brown sugar
Pinch of cayenne pepper

Combine the pecans, cashews and egg white in a bowl. Toss to coat. Add the cinnamon, brown sugar and cayenne pepper and mix well. Spread on a baking sheet. Bake at 350 degrees for 10 minutes. Stir, then bake 5 minutes longer.

Makes 8 to 10 servings

Alan Morestein, Regi's American Bistro

CANTALOUPE SOUP

4 cantaloupes, cut into halves crosswise
1¹/2 cups apple juice
2/3 cup sugar
1/2 cup sherry
1 tablespoon lemon juice
3/4 teaspoon ground ginger
3/4 teaspoon vanilla extract
Mint leaves
1 lime, sliced
Crème Fraîche (page 182)

Remove the seeds from the cantaloupes. Scoop out the cantaloupe, reserving the shells to use as bowls, if desired. Combine the cantaloupe, apple juice, sugar, sherry, lemon juice, ginger and vanilla in a blender or food processor. Process until smooth. Cover and chill the soup, stirring occasionally. Serve in the reserved cantaloupe shells or soup bowls. Garnish servings with mint leaves, lime slices and crème fraîche.

Makes 6 to 8 servings

Jane Sabatelli

Tip: *If using the cantaloupe shells as bowls, cut a thin slice from the bottom of each so it can sit flat. Use a spoon to smooth the inside of the shell to ensure an attractive presentation.*

Black Bean Salad with Fire-Roasted Tomatoes

4 ears of corn
1 (15-ounce) can black beans, drained and rinsed
1 tablespoon minced red onion
1 (15-ounce) can fire-roasted tomatoes
1/2 cup olive oil
1 tablespoon cider vinegar
Zest and juice of 1 lemon
Zest and juice of 1 lime
1/4 teaspoon cayenne pepper
1/4 teaspoon salt
1/2 teaspoon chipotle chili powder

Cook the corn in a large pan of boiling water for 3 to 4 minutes; drain. Let cool. Pat the corn dry. Cut the kernels from the cob with a sharp knife. You should have about 2 cups of corn kernels.

Toss the corn with the beans, onion, tomatoes, olive oil, vinegar, lemon zest, lemon juice, lime zest, lime juice, cayenne pepper, salt and chili powder.

Makes 8 servings

Tip: Serve as a side dish with grilled meat, poultry, or fish or serve on greens as a luncheon salad.

ROASTED BABY BEET SALAD

CITRUS DRESSING
1 orange
1 grapefruit
1 tablespoon honey
3/4 cup vegetable oil
1/3 cup balsamic vinegar
1/2 teaspoon kosher salt
1/2 teaspoon cracked pepper

SALAD
12 baby beets (golden or
   mixed colors)
1 garlic clove, minced
1/4 cup olive oil
1/2 teaspoon kosher salt
1/2 teaspoon pepper
1 avocado, sliced
5 ounces baby arugula
2 ounces chèvre, crumbled

For the dressing, zest the orange into a bowl. Cut off the peel and membrane and cut the orange sections away from the membrane. Work over the bowl to catch the juice. Squeeze the membrane to extract all the juice. Section a grapefruit in a similar manner. Add the citrus sections, honey, oil, vinegar, salt and pepper to the juices and mix well.

For the salad, wash and trim the beets. Cut the beets into halves. Combine with the garlic, olive oil, salt and pepper in a baking dish. Roast at 350 degrees for 20 to 30 minutes until tender. Combine the beets and 1/2 cup of the dressing in a bowl and toss to coat. (Recipe may be made to this point and left at room temperature for several hours or refrigerated until ready to serve.)

Add the avocado to the beets. Toss to coat with the dressing. Divide the arugula among 6 serving plates. Top with the beet salad. Drizzle with additional dressing. Sprinkle with the cheese.

Makes 6 servings

Tip: Beets are at their most flavorful served at room temperature.

Asian Cabbage Salad

Soy Dressing
$1/2$ cup sugar
$1/4$ cup rice vinegar
$3/4$ cup vegetable oil
2 tablespoons soy sauce

Salad
1 large head napa cabbage,
    thinly sliced

2 bunches green onions, sliced
    (white parts only)
2 packages ramen noodles,
    seasoning packet discarded
1 cup sliced or slivered almonds
2 tablespoons sesame seeds
$1/2$ cup (1 stick) butter

For the dressing, combine the sugar, vinegar, oil and soy sauce in a saucepan. Bring to a boil. Reduce the heat and simmer for 1 minute. Let cool completely.

For the salad, combine the cabbage and green onions in a bowl. Crush the noodles. Brown the noodles, almonds and sesame seeds in the butter in a skillet. Remove to a small bowl and let cool. Combine with the cabbage mixture. Pour the dressing over the salad and toss to coat. Refrigerate the salad for 1 hour before serving.

Makes 12 servings

Bruce Kirby

Tip: *Add chicken, shrimp, or roasted pork for a salad that's hearty enough to be an entrée.*

PICNIC COLESLAW

1 large head cabbage, shredded
1 onion, thinly sliced
3/4 cup sugar
1 cup white wine vinegar

1 teaspoon salt
1 teaspoon celery seeds
1 teaspoon dry mustard
1 cup vegetable oil

Layer the cabbage and onion in a large bowl. Sprinkle with the sugar; do not stir. Combine the vinegar, salt, celery seeds, dry mustard and oil in a saucepan. Bring to a boil. Let cool to room temperature. Pour the dressing over the salad; do not stir. Cover and refrigerate until serving time. Stir the slaw before serving.

Makes 6 to 8 servings

Hans Mayer

CAESAR SALAD

CAESAR DRESSING
4 anchovy fillets
2 garlic cloves, minced
3/4 cup light olive oil
2 tablespoons lemon juice
1 teaspoon Worcestershire sauce
1/2 cup bottled creamy Parmesan
   salad dressing

1 teaspoon Dijon mustard
Cracked black pepper to taste

SALAD
2 heads romaine
1/4 cup (1 ounce) shredded
   Parmesan cheese
Croutons (page 91)

For the dressing, combine the anchovies, garlic, olive oil, lemon juice, Worcestershire sauce, salad dressing, Dijon mustard and pepper in a food processor. Process until smooth and well blended.

For the salad, tear or cut the lettuce into bite-size pieces. Combine the lettuce and cheese in a salad bowl. Add the salad dressing and toss to coat. Top with Croutons.

Makes 8 servings

GRILLED CAESAR SALAD

1 head romaine
$1/2$ cup olive oil
Juice of 1 lemon
1 cup Caesar Dressing (page 48)
1 cup (4 ounces) shaved Parmesan cheese
$1/2$ cup kalamata olives
$1^1/2$ cups Croutons (page 91)
12 anchovy fillets

Trim the outer leaves and stem of the lettuce, removing any bruised or dark spots. Rinse. Do not separate leaves from core. Roll several paper towels around the lettuce. Chill. Preheat the grill. Combine the olive oil and lemon juice in a small dish. Cut the lettuce into quarters lengthwise, leaving the core intact so the leaves hold together. Brush the edges with the olive oil mixture. Grill on one of the cut sides for 45 seconds. Turn and grill the other cut side for 45 seconds.

Plate the grilled lettuce wedges. Drizzle with the Caesar Dressing. Top with the cheese, olives, Croutons and anchovies. Serve immediately.

Makes 4 servings

Tip: This salad is an example of a recent food trend known as "deconstructed." When served, each ingredient is presented individually allowing diners to "build their own bites."

Greek Salad

Red Wine and Tomato Vinaigrette
3/4 cup vegetable oil
1/4 cup red wine vinegar
1/4 cup vegetable juice cocktail
1/2 teaspoon pepper

Salad
3 heirloom tomatoes, mixed colors
1 seedless cucumber, sliced
1/2 red onion, sliced
1/2 cup kalamata olives, pitted
1 tablespoon capers
5 cups baby arugula
6 pepperoncini
1 cup crumbled feta cheese
Anchovies to taste

For the dressing, whisk the oil, vinegar, juice cocktail and pepper in a bowl until blended.

For the salad, core the tomatoes and chop into bite-size pieces. Combine in a large bowl with the cucumber, onion, olives, capers, arugula and pepperoncini. Toss with enough dressing to coat the leaves. Top with the feta and anchovies.

Makes 4 to 6 servings

Spinach Salad

Orange Honey Mustard Dressing
Zest and juice of 1 orange
2 tablespoons lemon juice
1 cup vegetable oil
1/4 teaspoon salt
1/4 teaspoon cracked pepper
1 tablespoon honey mustard

Salad
Sections of 1 orange
Sections of 1 grapefruit
1 avocado, sliced
5 ounces baby spinach
2 ounces chèvre, crumbled
1/2 cup dried cranberries
1/2 cup Candied Walnuts (page 180)

For the dressing, whisk the orange zest, orange juice, lemon juice, oil, salt, pepper and honey mustard together in a bowl. Refrigerate for up to 1 week.

For the salad, combine the orange, grapefruit and avocado in a bowl and toss gently. Add the spinach, cheese, cranberries and Candied Walnuts. Toss with enough dressing to coat the ingredients.

Makes 4 servings

CHESAPEAKE BAY SEAFOOD SALAD

SESAME VINAIGRETTE
3/4 cup vegetable oil
2 tablespoons sesame oil
1/4 cup rice wine vinegar
1/2 teaspoon cracked black pepper
1 teaspoon Dijon mustard

SEAFOOD SALAD
1 head romaine, chopped
1/4 cup kalamata olives, chopped
1/2 green bell pepper, julienned
1/2 red bell pepper, julienned
1/2 orange bell pepper, julienned
1/2 yellow bell pepper, julienned

1/2 Vidalia onion, julienned
1 pound jumbo shrimp, steamed,
    peeled and deveined
4 slices applewood-smoked bacon,
    crisp-cooked and crumbled
3/4 cup (3 ounces) grated
    Asiago cheese
4 hard-cooked eggs,
    cut into quarters
2 ounces jumbo lump crab meat
1/2 cup (2 ounces) grated
    Parmesan cheese
2 tablespoons sesame seeds, toasted

For the dressing, whisk the vegetable oil, sesame oil, vinegar, pepper and Dijon mustard together in a bowl.

For the salad, combine the lettuce, olives, bell peppers, onion, shrimp, bacon, Asiago cheese and egg in a large bowl. Add 3/4 cup of the dressing and toss to coat. Top with the crab meat. Sprinkle with the Parmesan cheese and sesame seeds. Serve with the remaining dressing.

Makes 4 servings

Bruce Dorsey, Metropolitan Café

Tip: Shrimp is sold both by the pound and by the count. The smaller the count, the larger the shrimp. For example, this recipe calls for "jumbo shrimp," which come about twelve to the pound.

APPLE NUT SALAD

2 large Red Delicious apples
2 teaspoons lemon juice
1/2 cup salted peanuts
1/4 cup raisins

2 tablespoons mayonnaise
1 tablespoon plus 1 teaspoon
  honey

Core the apples and chop into bite-size pieces. Combine with the lemon juice in a bowl and toss to coat. Add the peanuts, raisins, mayonnaise and honey and mix well.

Makes 4 servings

Mary Lou Mullen

WATERMELON AND BLUE CHEESE SALAD

3 cups seedless watermelon cubes
Sections of 2 oranges
1 tablespoon chopped parsley
Zest and juice of 1 lime
Juice of 1 lemon

1/2 cup vegetable oil
1/2 teaspoon kosher salt
Cracked pepper to taste
3/4 cup crumbled blue cheese
Bibb lettuce

Combine the watermelon, orange and parsley in a large bowl. Whisk the lime juice, lime zest, lemon juice and oil in a small bowl. Add the salt and pepper. Serve the salad topped with the blue cheese and lightly tossed with a little dressing.
Serve on Bibb lettuce or in porcelain spoons as an amuse bouche.

Makes 6 servings

Tip: In French, *"amuse bouche" means "happy mouth."*
It is often served as a small surprise from the chef to enhance the meal, or it may be served as an hors d'oeuvre.

LOBSTER GRILLED CHEESE

LOBSTER
1 (12-ounce) bottle beer
1 teaspoon sea salt
1 tablespoon Old Bay seasoning
1 quart (4 cups) water
2 (6- to 8-ounce) lobster tails

SANDWICH ASSEMBLY
2 tablespoons butter, softened
8 slices boule or other round crusty French bread
4 to 6 ounces Chaumes or Port Salut cheese, sliced into strips
Zest of 1 lemon
White pepper to taste

For the lobster, combine the beer, salt, Old Bay seasoning and water in a stockpot with a tight-fitting lid. Bring to a boil. Add the lobster tails. Cover and steam for 5 to 6 minutes. Remove the lobster and cool. Split the shells and remove the meat. Slice into medallions.

For the sandwiches, lightly butter one side of each bread slice. Layer half the cheese on the unbuttered sides of half the slices. Layer the lobster evenly over the cheese. Sprinkle each with lemon zest and white pepper. Top with the remaining cheese and bread, buttered sides up.

Grill the sandwiches in a heavy skillet until brown on both sides, turning once.

Makes 4 servings

Tip: Chaumes is a cow's milk cheese with a mellow, nutty taste and mild aroma. It is milder than Muenster and not as strong as Port Salut.

GRILLED SALMON WRAPS WITH STRAWBERRY JALAPEÑO BARBECUE SAUCE

SALMON
1 (12-ounce) can beer
1/4 cup maple syrup
1/4 cup canola oil
1 tablespoon Old Bay seasoning
1 pound salmon fillet, skin off

WRAP ASSEMBLY
4 ounces cream cheese, softened
3 flatbreads
1 cup Strawberry Jalapeño Barbecue Sauce (page 185)
2 cups mixed field greens
1/4 cup coleslaw dressing

For the salmon, combine the beer, maple syrup, canola oil and Old Bay seasoning in a bowl. Pour over the salmon in a baking dish. Marinate for 30 minutes. Prepare a medium-hot fire on the grill. Coat the grate with oil or nonstick cooking spray. Grill the salmon for 4 to 5 minutes on each side.

For the wrap, spread cream cheese on half of one side of each flatbread. (The cream cheese holds the wrap together.) Bring the barbecue sauce to a boil in a small saucepan. Pour the sauce over the salmon in a dish or platter. Break the salmon into pieces and lay across the center of the flatbread. Top with greens. Drizzle with the dressing.

Roll to enclose the filling. Tuck in the top edge to make a firm wrap. Cut the wraps on the diagonal.

Makes 6 servings

Chesapeake Oyster Po' Boys

Caper Mayonnaise
1 tablespoon capers, chopped
1/2 cup mayonnaise
1 teaspoon lemon zest
1 tablespoon lemon juice
1 tablespoon chopped parsley

Oysters and Assembly
24 oysters
1/2 cup cornmeal
1 cup vegetable oil
6 fresh hoagie rolls
1 head romaine, shredded
2 Roma tomatoes, diced
Salt and pepper to taste
1 teaspoon Old Bay seasoning

For the mayonnaise, combine the capers, mayonnaise, lemon zest, lemon juice and parsley in a small bowl; mix well.

For the sandwiches, coat the oysters with the cornmeal. Fry in the hot oil in a skillet until golden brown. Drain on paper towels. Keep warm.

Toast the hoagie rolls. Spread the rolls with the caper mayonnaise. Pile lettuce and tomatoes evenly onto the rolls. Top each with 4 oysters; season with salt, pepper and Old Bay seasoning.

Makes 6 servings

Chef Ronald Robinson, Harbor Court Hotel

QUESADILLAS WITH PULLED PORK AND CHIPOTLE SWEET POTATOES

PORK AND SWEET POTATOES
2 sweet potatoes
1 teaspoon chipotle chili powder
1 (1-pound) pork tenderloin
1/2 teaspoon salt
1 teaspoon garlic pepper
1 tablespoon olive oil
1 tablespoon lime juice
1/4 cup water

CRISP FLOUR TORTILLAS
1/2 cup (about) canola oil
8 (8-inch) flour tortillas

QUESADILLA ASSEMBLY
2 cups (8 ounces) shredded Pepper
    Jack cheese
2 cups (8 ounces) shredded
    Cheddar cheese
1/2 cup sour cream
1/2 cup Fresh Salsa (recipe page 24)

For the pork and sweet potatoes, pierce the sweet potatoes with a knife or fork. Arrange on a baking pan. Bake at 350 degrees for 45 minutes or until tender. Let cool slightly. Peel the potatoes and then mash in a bowl with the chili powder.

Season the pork with the salt and garlic pepper. Sauté in the olive oil in a roasting pan over high heat until brown. Add the lime juice and cook for several minutes. Add the water, cover the pan and bake at 350 degrees for 25 minutes or until the tenderloin registers 145 degrees on a meat thermometer. Remove from the oven. Let stand, covered, for 30 minutes. Shred the pork. Drizzle with any pan juices. (The pork may be prepared to this point up to a day in advance and refrigerated.)

For the tortillas, pour about half the canola oil in a skillet large enough for a tortilla to lie flat. Heat the oil. Add a tortilla. Brown for 1 minute. Turn and brown for 1 minute longer. Drain on paper towels. Cook all the tortillas in a similar manner, adding more oil as needed. (Tortillas may be fried several hours in advance.)

To assemble the quesadillas, spread the half the cheeses evenly over half the tortillas. Top evenly with the pork. Add a dollop of the mashed sweet potatoes. Top with the remaining cheeses, then a second tortilla.

Bake at 350 degrees for 15 to 20 minutes until the cheese melts and the quesadillas are warm. Let stand 5 minutes. Cut into wedges. Top each wedge with sour cream and salsa to serve.

Makes 4 servings

Tip: It is not necessary to "flip" this quesadilla. All the ingredients may be prepared ahead of time. Pre-fried crisp tortillas hold up well and keep their crunch when filled and finished in the oven.

GRILLED EGGPLANT AND MUENSTER ON CIABATTA

EGGPLANT
2 large eggplant
3/4 cup olive oil
1/4 cup balsamic vinegar
1 teaspoon mayonnaise
1/2 teaspoon chopped garlic
1/2 teaspoon salt
1/2 teaspoon pepper

ASSEMBLY
1 avocado, sliced (optional)
1 tablespoon olive oil
Zest of 1 lemon
1 tablespoon lemon juice
6 ciabatta rolls
1/2 cup hummus
6 slices Muenster cheese
1 (8-ounce) can water chestnuts, drained and sliced
6 slices fire-roasted bell peppers
3 cups mixed field greens

For the eggplant, cut the unpeeled eggplant into 1/2-inch-thick rounds. Combine the olive oil, vinegar, mayonnaise, garlic, salt and pepper in a shallow dish. Coat each eggplant round with the olive oil mixture. Arrange on a rimmed sheet pan. Let stand for 15 to 30 minutes.

Grill the eggplant over direct heat for 2 to 3 minutes on each side. Return the eggplant to the sheet pan. (Eggplant may be prepared several hours in advance. Reheat in a warm oven or serve at room temperature.)

For the sandwiches, combine the avocado, olive oil, lemon zest and lemon juice in a bowl. Cut the ciabatta into halves horizontally. Spread with hummus. Layer a slice of cheese, two pieces of the eggplant, the water chestnuts, avocado, bell peppers and field greens on the bottom slice. Add the top slice of bread. Cut the sandwich into halves to serve.

Makes 6 sandwiches

Tip: Grilling eggplant does not require an outdoor grill. A panini press, cast-iron skillet, or oven broiler works well for cooking indoors. Be sure to use your stove's exhaust, as cooking eggplant can create a lot of smoke.

TURKEY BURGERS

2 tablespoons minced yellow onion
2 tablespoons minced red bell pepper
1 pound turkey breast, ground
1 tablespoon minced chipotle chile
1 tablespoon honey
1 teaspoon lemon juice
1/4 cup panko (Japanese bread crumbs)
Salt and pepper to taste
4 kaiser rolls

Sauté the onion and bell pepper in a skillet until caramelized. Combine with the turkey, chipotle chile, honey, lemon juice, panko, salt and pepper in a bowl and mix well. Form into four patties. Cook on a flat-top grill for 5 minutes per side until the patties register 165 degrees on a meat thermometer. Serve on the rolls with your favorite toppings.

Makes 4 servings

Alan Morestein, Regi's American Bistro

Tip: Onions caramelize because of their natural sugars. Sautéing them over medium-high heat results in a lovely caramel color and taste.

PIMENTO CHEESE, ROASTED RED PEPPER AND PINE NUT SPREAD

1 cup pine nuts
1 teaspoon olive oil
Pinch of salt
1 pound sharp Cheddar cheese, shredded
2 large roasted red peppers, peeled and minced
1 tablespoon Tiger sauce
3/4 cup mayonnaise
1/2 cup Durkee sauce
Crostini (page 91)

Combine the pine nuts, olive oil and salt. Spread on a sheet pan. Bake at 350 degrees for 5 minutes, checking frequently. Let cool.

Combine the cheese, peppers, Tiger sauce, mayonnaise and Durkee sauce in a bowl. Add the pine nuts. Serve on crostini or as a filling for tea sandwiches.

Makes 6 servings

*Tip: Turn this spread into a hot hors d'oeuvre.
Top Crostini (page 91) with the spread, then bake for
several minutes until warm.*

Lisa Egeli

*"When I had nowhere to go and no one to help me,
I arrived at the shelter. The shelter manager told me that
my children and I were going to be okay. They would help me.
It was a process, and they were there each step of the way with me.
I am very appreciative of their help."*

Latoya

Former resident, living in independent housing

BOS Homeless Shelter

Imagine losing your job and then being evicted from your apartment with your two children. There is no one in your family nor are there friends who have enough money to help you keep your housing. Everything you own is put out on the street. You don't have a car or any money for a storage unit, so all you can do is gather a few garbage bags that you can pull along with you as you get on a bus. Your kids don't understand what is happening — why they are being put out of their home or why you are leaving most of your belongings on the street. They want all their toys, but you can't carry them. They can only keep a few things. The children are crying, and you are embarrassed that your life has come to this.

For the next month, you try staying with different family members and friends a few days at a time, but they do not have room for you, and they are afraid that they will get evicted for having people living with them that are not supposed to be there. After a month of trying to keep your children housed, you become so desperate that you are willing to go to an emergency shelter — you have no place left to go. You find Baltimore City Homeless Services, and they tell you to go line up at one of the shelters so you can get a bed for the night. In the morning you have to go to the day program. There is not a place to keep the few belongings you have left.

Most of our clients share a journey similar to the one above. They have been homeless for several months to a year before they arrive. The staff, many of whom are former shelter residents, developed the shelter to be a home. Having lived here, they know how it feels to walk into a forty-bed dorm-style community for the first time. Each resident has her own dresser and bed that are hers as long as she lives here. Everyone contributes by completing a chore each week. A community forms as everyone struggles to have a better life. The twenty children have friends to play with. Often older women help younger women. Gone is the need to line up for a bed that night — once you are accepted, you are home. Most emergency shelters in the Baltimore area limit residents to a ninety-day stay. The residents at BOS stay in our emergency shelter until housing is available, provided they are working toward their goals of housing and self sufficiency. Since there are few opportunities for families with low incomes, most families stay in the BOS shelter for six months until a housing opportunity becomes available.

PERFECT FAMILY SUPPER

Menu

Roasted Baby Beet Salad

❖

Pork Tenderloin with Mushroom Wine Sauce

❖

Pan-Seared Haricots Verts

❖

Corn Pudding

❖

Carrot Cake with Cream Cheese Frosting

*Make sure the special supper with family and friends is
planned so that it is fun for the cook. It's the perfect time for everyone
to come together and share the day. To be sure the cook doesn't
miss the conversation, everything on this menu can be prepared ahead
and finished in the oven or microwave about
20 minutes before serving*

GRILLED ASPARAGUS

2 pounds asparagus, trimmed
1/2 cup olive oil
Juice and zest of 1 lemon
Sea salt and cracked pepper to taste

Boil the asparagus in water to cover in a saucepan for 1 minute; drain. Plunge the asparagus into ice water to stop the cooking process. Drain and pat dry.

Coat the asparagus with 1/4 cup of the olive oil in a shallow dish, taking care not to break the tips. Grill directly on the grate or use a grill pan long enough for marks to appear.

Remove to a serving platter. Drizzle with the remaining 1/4 cup olive oil. Sprinkle with lemon zest, lemon juice, salt and pepper.

Makes 6 to 8 servings

PAN-SEARED HARICOTS VERTS

1 shallot, minced
2 tablespoons Garlic-Infused Oil (page 184)
1 pound haricots verts (baby green beans)
1 cup chicken stock
2 tablespoons roasted red pepper, chopped
1 tablespoon butter
Salt and pepper to taste

Sauté the shallot in the infused oil until translucent. Add the green beans. Sauté for 1 minute. Add the stock. Simmer, covered, for 8 to 10 minutes. Remove the beans to a serving platter. Simmer the cooking liquid, uncovered, until reduced to 1/3 cup. Add the red pepper, butter, salt and pepper. Remove from the heat and stir to blend. Pour the sauce over the beans.

Makes 6 servings

Brussels Sprouts with Marmalade Glaze

1¹/2 pounds Brussels sprouts
1 shallot, minced
2 tablespoons butter
¹/2 cup orange marmalade
Zest and juice of 1 lemon
1 tablespoon cider vinegar
Salt and pepper to taste

Prepare the Brussels sprouts by removing blemished leaves and trimming the stems. Cut an "X" in the stems with a paring knife.

Bring water to a rapid boil in a large pan. Add the Brussels sprouts. Cover, reduce the heat and cook until tender; drain.

Sauté the shallot in the butter in a saucepan. Add the marmalade, lemon zest, lemon juice and vinegar. Simmer until the marmalade melts. Add the Brussels sprouts and stir to coat. Season with salt and pepper. Heat through.

Makes 6 servings

Carrot Pudding

5 pounds carrots, peeled
and chopped
1 teaspoon salt
²/3 cup sugar
1 cup (2 sticks) butter,
at room temperature
2 tablespoons plus
2 teaspoons flour
Pinch of cinnamon
1 quart (4 cups) milk
12 eggs, beaten
1 tablespoon baking powder

Cook the carrots in boiling water in a stockpot until tender; drain. Purée the carrots in a food processor. Add the salt, sugar and butter and mix well. Add the flour, cinnamon, milk, eggs and baking powder and mix well. Pour into a baking dish. Bake at 350 degrees for 1 hour or until a knife inserted in the pudding comes out clean.

Makes 10 to 12 servings

Marlene Meyer

CAULIFLOWER WITH CHIVES

1 head cauliflower	2 tablespoons butter
Salt to taste	1 teaspoon white pepper
1/2 cup milk	1/2 teaspoon dry mustard
8 ounces cream cheese	1 tablespoon chopped chives

Trim the cauliflower. Break into florets. (A medium head of cauliflower should yield about 4 cups florets.) Boil the cauliflower in salted water in a medium saucepan for 10 to 15 minutes until tender; drain.

Combine the milk, cream cheese and butter in a medium saucepan. Simmer for several minutes or until well combined, stirring frequently. Add the white pepper, dry mustard, salt and chives. Add the cauliflower and stir to coat.

Makes 6 servings

This variation on a traditional British vegetable is often served instead of potatoes or as a luncheon entrée with a crisp salad and crusty bread.

CORN PUDDING

3/4 cup (1 1/2 sticks) butter	1/4 cup yellow cornmeal
3 (15-ounce) cans cream-style corn	2 teaspoons baking powder
1 (12-ounce) can evaporated milk	1 teaspoon white pepper
1 tablespoon sugar	1 teaspoon salt
8 eggs, beaten	

Melt the butter in a baking dish in a 350-degree oven. Maintain the oven temperature. Combine the corn, evaporated milk, sugar, eggs, cornmeal, baking powder, white pepper and salt in a bowl and mix well. Pour into the baking dish. Bake for 1 hour.

Makes 10 to 12 servings

Eggplant Soufflé

Juice of 1 lemon
3 eggplant, peeled and cubed
1 teaspoon salt
34 butter crackers, crushed
3 eggs, beaten
1/4 cup milk

2 tablespoons dried onion flakes
Pepper to taste
12 ounces Velveeta cheese, cubed
7 slices bacon, cooked and
    crumbled

Combine the lemon juice with ice water in a large bowl to prevent the eggplant from turning brown. Peel and cube the eggplant. Add to the ice water; drain.

Boil the eggplant in salted water in a large saucepan until tender; drain. Mash the eggplant in a large mixing bowl. Add the cracker crumbs, eggs, milk, onion flakes and pepper and mix well. Spoon into a well-greased baking pan. Press the cheese cubes into the mixture, distributing them evenly. Sprinkle with the bacon.

Bake at 350 degrees for 30 minutes.

Makes 6 to 8 servings

Lesley Miller

Baked Vidalia Onions

2 Vidalia onions
1 tablespoon light olive oil
Kosher salt to taste
1 teaspoon white pepper, or
    to taste

1 1/2 cups heavy cream
1/4 cup (1 ounce) grated
    Parmesan cheese
1 1/2 cups (6 ounces) shredded
    sharp white Cheddar cheese

Slice the top and bottom off each onion to make a flat surface. Cut into halves. Brush the onions with the olive oil. Season with salt and the white pepper. Arrange the onions in a baking dish. Bake at 375 degrees for 25 minutes or until translucent. Maintain the oven temperature. Pour the cream over the onions. Sprinkle with the Parmesan cheese. Top with the Cheddar cheese. Season with additional salt and white pepper.

Bake for 20 minutes longer or until the cream is bubbly and cheese is melted and light brown.

Makes 4 servings

STUFFED RED PEPPERS

1 1/2 pounds tomatoes, chopped
1/2 cup basil, chopped
1 garlic clove, chopped
3 small anchovy fillets, chopped
3 sun-dried tomatoes, chopped

2 teaspoons balsamic vinegar
3 tablespoons olive oil
4 large red bell peppers,
   cut into halves

Combine the tomatoes, basil, garlic, anchovies and sun-dried tomatoes in a bowl and mix well. Add the vinegar and olive oil and mix well. Spoon into the bell pepper halves. Arrange in a baking dish. Bake at 400 degrees for 40 minutes. Serve warm or at room temperature.

Makes 8 servings

Gail Shawe

POTATOES AU GRATIN

8 large red skin potatoes,
   thinly sliced
Salt to taste
16 ounces cream cheese, chopped
1 cup chicken stock
1 cup half-and-half
1 cup heavy cream

1 cup (4 ounces) grated
   Parmesan cheese
4 cups (16 ounces) shredded
   Cheddar cheese
1/2 teaspoon salt
1/2 tablespoon white pepper
Pinch of nutmeg

Boil the potatoes in salted water for 1 minute; drain. Cover in ice water until cool; drain well. Let stand until completely dry.

Melt the cream cheese with the stock in a saucepan, stirring to blend. Add the half-and-half and mix well. Add the cream, Parmesan cheese, $3^{2/3}$ cups of the Cheddar cheese, the salt, white pepper and nutmeg. Simmer until the cheese melts and sauce is thick and creamy. Let cool to room temperature.

Grease a large baking dish. Layer the potatoes, slightly overlapping, to cover the bottom of the dish. Cover with a small amount of sauce. Repeat the layers, ending with sauce. Bake at 350 degrees for 35 to 45 minutes. Sprinkle with the remaining 1/3 cup Cheddar cheese. Bake for 10 minutes longer. Let stand for 15 to 20 minutes.

Makes 8 servings

RED BLISS POTATO SALAD

3 pounds red skin potatoes, diced
1/4 cup sweet pickle relish
2 cups mayonnaise
1/2 tablespoon Dijon mustard
1/2 tablespoon yellow mustard

1 teaspoon salt
1/4 teaspoon pepper
1/2 teaspoon celery seeds
1 cup diced celery
3 hard-boiled eggs, roughly chopped

Boil the unpeeled potatoes in water to cover in a saucepan until tender; drain. Let cool.

Combine the relish, mayonnaise, Dijon mustard, yellow mustard, salt, pepper and celery seeds. Spoon the potatoes into a serving bowl. Add the dressing, celery and eggs and mix well.

Makes 8 to 10 servings

POTATO LATKES

6 russet potatoes, peeled
3 small onions
1 tablespoon lemon juice
4 eggs

1/4 cup all-purpose flour
1 teaspoon salt
1/2 teaspoon pepper
Vegetable oil for frying

Grate the potatoes and onions into a large bowl. Drain the starchy liquid that collects at the bottom of the bowl.

Combine the lemon juice, eggs, flour, salt and pepper in a bowl and mix well. Add to the potato mixture and mix well. Form into thin patties. Fry the patties in hot oil in a skillet until golden brown on both sides. Drain on paper towels.

Makes 10 to 12 servings

Alan Morestein, Regi's American Bistro

Oven-Roasted Potatoes

Fingerling potatoes can be used instead of red potatoes. Other vegetables such as squash and beets may be roasted and added to the mix for color and flavor, so take advantage of produce in season.

6 red skin potatoes, unpeeled
4 sweet potatoes, peeled
1 cup Garlic-Infused Oil (page 184)
1 teaspoon kosher salt
1 onion, chopped

Cut the potatoes and sweet potatoes into bite-size pieces, but keep them separate.

Pour 1/2 cup of the infused oil into a bowl, making sure to include some of the garlic and herbs from the oil. Add the red potatoes and toss to coat.

Spread the red potatoes on a baking sheet. Sprinkle with 1/2 teaspoon of the salt. Roast at 350 degrees for 30 to 40 minutes until the potatoes are tender, checking and stirring after 15 minutes.

Toss the sweet potatoes and onion with the remaining 1/2 cup infused oil. Spread on a baking sheet. Roast at 350 for 20 to 30 minutes until tender. Toss with the red potatoes and serve.

Makes 6 to 8 servings

Tip: To prevent discoloration when peeling or cutting potatoes, put them into cold water until ready to cook.

Spinach and Artichoke Casserole

1 (14-ounce) can artichoke hearts, drained and cut into halves
3 (10-ounce) packages frozen chopped spinach
8 ounces cream cheese
1/4 cup chicken broth
1/4 teaspoon garlic salt
1/4 teaspoon salt
1/8 teaspoon pepper
1 cup sour cream
2 tablespoons grated Parmesan cheese

Coat a 1-quart baking dish with nonstick cooking spray. Arrange the artichokes in the dish. Cook the spinach according to the package directions; drain well.

Combine the spinach, cream cheese, broth, garlic salt, salt, pepper and sour cream in a large skillet. Heat until the cream cheese melts, stirring to mix well. Spoon over the artichokes. Sprinkle with the Parmesan cheese. Bake at 350 degrees for 30 minutes or until bubbly.

Makes 6 servings

Betty Higman

Wilted Spinach with Brown Garlic

10 ounces fresh spinach
5 garlic cloves, minced
1/4 cup olive oil
1/2 teaspoon sea salt
2 dashes of Tabasco sauce
1/4 teaspoon nutmeg
1 tablespoon butter, softened
Salt and pepper to taste
Pepperoncini to taste

Remove any large stems from the spinach leaves. Rinse the spinach well, then drain thoroughly.

Sauté the garlic in the olive oil until light brown, stirring constantly and watching carefully to prevent overbrowning. Add the spinach a little at a time and cook until wilted but still bright green, turning with tongs and adding more spinach gradually. Add the salt, Tabasco sauce and nutmeg.

Remove the spinach to a serving bowl using a slotted spoon. Add the butter and mix well. Season with salt, pepper and pepperoncini.

Makes 4 servings

SPAGHETTI SQUASH WITH SUN-DRIED TOMATOES AND TOASTED PINE NUTS

1 spaghetti squash, cut into halves
1/4 cup olive oil
1/2 cup pine nuts
1 tablespoon olive oil
1 tablespoon chopped shallot
1 garlic clove, minced

3 tablespoons olive oil
1 cup oil-pack sun-dried tomatoes, drained and julienned
2 tablespoons tomato paste
1 cup chicken stock
2 tablespoons butter, softened

Scoop the seeds from the squash. Rub the squash with 1/4 cup olive oil. Arrange cut side down on a foil-covered rimmed baking sheet. Pour in 1 cup water. Bake at 350 degrees for 30 to 40 minutes until the squash is tender. Let cool. When cool, use a fork to pull the squash from the shell.

Toast the pine nuts in 1 tablespoon olive oil in a skillet until light brown, stirring constantly.

Sauté the shallot and garlic in 3 tablespoons olive oil for 2 to 3 minutes. Add the sun-dried tomatoes, tomato paste and stock. Cook until the liquid is reduced by one-third. Remove from the heat. Add the butter and squash and toss to combine. Sprinkle with the pine nuts to serve.

Makes 4 servings

Tip: To cut any hard-shelled squash, microwave the squash on High for about 2 minutes. This softens the shell, making it much easier to cut.

As students learn to prepare unfamiliar foods, they often react with, "I don't eat that." Lunch hour is a time to share the food they've prepared, especially if it's unfamiliar. Knowing that wilted spinach, eggplant, and spaghetti squash are now on the list of foods they'd like to share with their families makes it a good day! —The Chef

Baked Squash

4 zucchini squash, cut into
1/4-inch rounds
4 yellow squash, cut into
1/4-inch rounds
Salt and white pepper to taste
1/2 cup (1 stick) butter
3/4 cup sour cream

1 white onion, diced
1/4 cup panko
(Japanese bread crumbs)
1 cup (4 ounces) shredded
Cheddar cheese
1 teaspoon parsley, chopped

Steam the squash in a steamer basket set over boiling water in a large pan for 3 to 4 minutes until tender-crisp. Drain, then pat dry. Season with salt and white pepper. Continue draining while preparing the sauce.

Melt the butter in a saucepan or microwave-safe bowl. Stir in the sour cream. Add the onion. Combine the panko, cheese and parsley in a bowl. Toss to combine. Layer half of the squash in a baking dish. Drizzle with one-third of the sauce. Layer on the remaining squash. Top with the remaining sauce. Sprinkle with the panko mixture. Bake at 350 degrees for 35 to 40 minutes. Serve hot.

Makes 6 to 8 servings

Tomato Pudding

1 (29-ounce) can tomato purée
1/2 cup dark brown sugar
Salt to taste

8 slices bread, cubed
6 tablespoons butter, melted

Heat the tomato purée and brown sugar in a saucepan. Season with salt. Bring to a simmer. Arrange the bread over the bottom of a greased baking dish. Pour the butter over the bread and toss to coat. Pour the tomato mixture over the bread. Let stand until the bread absorbs the liquid. Bake at 375 degrees for 30 minutes.

Makes 6 to 8 servings

Pat Himmelrich

FRIED GREEN TOMATOES

4 or 5 green tomatoes   Salt and pepper to taste
1 cup white cornmeal   1/2 cup vegetable oil

Core the tomatoes. Trim the curved top and bottom to create flat slices. Cut the tomato into 1/2-inch slices. Pour the cornmeal into a shallow dish. Season with salt and pepper and mix well. Coat each tomato slice with the cornmeal. Arrange the slices on a baking sheet. Refrigerate for 1 hour so the cornmeal can absorb the tomato liquid.

Heat the oil in a heavy skillet. Brown the tomatoes on each side. Drain on paper towels. Keep warm in a low oven.

Makes 6 servings

*Tip: Serve Fried Green Tomatoes as a side dish with almost any
entrée, or use them as a unique first course. Fan two slices of
Fried Green Tomato on mixed field greens. Sprinkle with feta cheese.
Top with jumbo lump crab meat. Drizzle with olive oil and
balsamic vinegar. Garnish with crumbled cooked bacon.*

STUFFED TOMATOES

3 large tomatoes   1 tablespoon vegetable oil
1 garlic clove, minced   Salt and white pepper to taste
1 yellow bell pepper, cut into strips   8 ounces Monterey Jack cheese,
12 portobello mushrooms,   shredded
   cut into strips   1 cup Béchamel Sauce (page 182)

Cut a slice from the bottom of each tomato so it will stand securely. Cut out the cores. Sauté the garlic, bell pepper and mushrooms in the oil in a skillet over high heat for 2 minutes or until tender-crisp. Season with salt and white pepper.

Fill the tomatoes with the pepper mixture. Sprinkle half the cheese over the tomatoes. Top with the Béchamel Sauce, then sprinkle with the remaining cheese.

Bake at 350 degrees for 25 to 30 minutes until the sauce is hot and bubbly. Serve with crusty bread as a first course or as a side dish.

Makes 6 servings

BRUNCH & BREADS

Hai-Ou Hou

"BOS helped me create a plan and work that plan to go from where I was to where I wanted to be. It was a process that took time, but I went from feeling hopeless and depressed to having hope and knowing that I had goals and seeing that I was making progress toward those goals."

Jackie

Former resident, current staff

BOS staff designed the shelter's programming to address the range of issues that lead to homelessness. In the process, BOS developed a structured program of rules as well as educational and counseling programs.

Losing housing, domestic violence, job loss, and the resulting financial difficulties are common stressful experiences that precede homelessness. In addition, some women experience significant mental health issues. We contracted with a licensed therapist who meets on site with the women. Residents see other women receiving counseling, which helps with the stigma of mental health treatment. Thirty-five percent of the residents have substance abuse issues, so we began testing residents and requiring treatment for substance abuse if a woman tests positive.

Many of our residents have been victims of domestic violence, so it is important that our shelter be a safe place. To reinforce safety, we established a policy of no hitting. Since most of our residents were raised with physical discipline,

we needed to teach other ways of disciplining children. Weekly parenting classes taught by a licensed social worker became a part of our program. The parenting classes have developed into a lively interchange of ideas and support for each other.

We also established financial planning as an important program element. Most of our residents have very little money. When they do acquire money, the impulse is often to spend it immediately, because there are so many needs. Classes address essential planning such as figuring out how many diapers are needed for the whole month and buying those first as well as exploring emotional triggers for spending.

BOS has a full-time caseworker that meets with each family weekly. The caseworker connects the women to resources they need—health care, mental health, family planning, and financial resources. In addition, women are referred to all of the housing opportunities that they qualify for and are helped to fill out applications.

Menu

Cranberry Orange Scones

Zucchini Bread with whipped butter and Blackberry Jam

Fresh Strawberries with Crème Fraîche

Asparagus and Rotel Frittata

Caramelized Bacon Breadsticks

Stuffed Baby Bella Mushrooms

❖

Moravian Sugar Cake

*When it's time to invite a crowd, brunch is a great option.
Special breads, scones, and coffee cakes are comfort foods
that offer a choice for everyone.*

*To invite a person into your house is to take charge of his happiness
for as long as he is under your roof.* —Brillat Savarin

CREPES CHAMPIGNON

CREPES
4 eggs
1 cup milk
1 tablespoon clarified butter
1 1/4 cups all-purpose flour
1 teaspoon salt
2 tablespoons vegetable oil

FILLING
2 cups mushrooms, sliced
1 tablespoon minced shallot
1/2 cup diced yellow bell pepper
1 tablespoon butter
Salt and pepper to taste
2 cups (8 ounces) shredded
 Gruyère cheese
2 cups Béchamel Sauce (page 182)

Combine the eggs, milk and butter in a medium bowl. Whisk to blend. Stir in the flour and salt. Chill in the refrigerator for up to 8 hours. Strain the batter. It should be the consistency of heavy cream.

Coat a nonstick crepe pan with a very small amount of the oil. Set it on the burner to heat. Ladle 1/4 cup of the batter into a corner of the pan. Tilt and quickly rotate the pan to cover the bottom with a thin layer of batter. Cook for about 1 minute. Turn and cook 30 to 40 seconds longer. Repeat with the remaining batter, adding oil to the pan as needed.

For the filling, sauté the mushrooms, shallot and bell pepper in the butter until tender. Season with salt and pepper. Let cool. Drain, reserving 1 tablespoon of the liquid.

Toss the mushroom mixture with the cheese. Add the reserved liquid; toss lightly. Spoon a small amount of the mushroom mixture into each crepe. Roll to enclose the filling. Arrange crepes snugly in a baking dish. Top with the Béchamel Sauce. Bake at 350 degrees for 15 to 20 minutes.

Makes 1 1/2 dozen crepes

Tip: To clarify butter, melt 1/2 cup (1 stick) of butter over medium-high heat until it begins to foam. Turn off the heat. Use a small spoon to skim the foam from the top. Discard the foam. The purpose of clarifying butter is to remove the milk solids, which burn at a high temperature, so that the butter can be used for high-heat cooking.

ASPARAGUS AND ROTEL FRITTATA

*In Spain, frittatas are served as tapas, or "little bites." They often include
sausages, potatoes, mushrooms, vegetables, and cheese.*

1 1/2 cups chopped asparagus
2 teaspoons olive oil
1 (10-ounce) can Rotel tomatoes with green chiles
1 (8-ounce) can water chestnuts, sliced
7 eggs
1/4 cup milk
1/4 teaspoon red pepper flakes
1/2 teaspoon kosher salt
1 cup (4 ounces) shredded sharp white Cheddar cheese
1/2 cup (2 ounces) grated Parmesan cheese

Sauté the asparagus in the olive oil in an ovenproof skillet. Add the tomatoes with green chiles and water chestnuts. Simmer for several minutes or until the liquid is reduced.

Combine the eggs, milk, pepper flakes and salt in a bowl. Whisk to combine. Pour over the asparagus in the skillet. Add the cheese. Cook until the sides begin to set.

Bake at 350 degrees for 20 minutes or until set and light brown. Let stand for several minutes. Cut into wedges.

Makes 6 servings

Note: *In addition to a starring role at breakfast, frittatas are
delicious served with salad for lunch or dinner.*

MAGIC OMELETS

*This is an easy way to make omelets for a group and allows guests
to choose their ingredients themselves. Be sure to have enough pots of
water boiling to allow the bags to move freely in the water.*

8 eggs
Salt and pepper to taste
1 cup diced ham
1 cup sautéed sliced onion
1 cup grape tomatoes, cut into halves
1 cup mushrooms, sautéed and drained
1 1/4 cups (5 ounces) shredded cheese

Bring a large stockpot half-full of water to a boil. Place a heavy-duty sealable bag into a 2-cup measure to support it. Break two eggs into the bag. Season with salt and pepper. Seal the bag. Remove from the cup and squeeze to break the yolks and mix the eggs.

Return the bag to the cup. Add 1 tablespoon of the ham, 1 tablespoon of the onion, 1 tablespoon of the tomatoes, 1 tablespoon of the mushrooms and 1 tablespoon of the cheese to the eggs. Seal the bag, pressing out the air. Drop the bag into the water. Cook for 10 minutes. The omelet will appear to be sticking to the sides of the bag at first, but will come together near the end of the cooking time.

Makes 4 servings

Tip: *Get all the ingredients chopped and ready
ahead of time so that it's easy for each guest to create his or
her own perfect omelet.*

ITALIAN STRATA

2 teaspoons chopped rosemary
2 teaspoons chopped thyme leaves
2 teaspoons chopped parsley
2 tablespoons olive oil
2 tablespoons butter
1/4 cup chopped zucchini
1/4 cup cremini mushrooms, chopped
5 eggs, beaten

1 cup milk
1 cup half-and-half
Salt and pepper to taste
1/2 loaf rustic bread, cubed
2 1/2 cups (10 ounces) shredded Italian cheese blend
3 cups crumbled goat cheese
1/2 cup chopped tomatoes

Sauté the rosemary, thyme and parsley in the olive oil and butter in a sauté pan for 1 to 2 minutes to infuse the oil with the herbs' flavors. Add the zucchini and mushrooms. Cook for 3 to 4 minutes until the vegetables are tender-crisp. Remove from the heat.

Combine the eggs, milk, half-and-half, salt and pepper in a medium bowl. Whisk to blend.

Set up the *mise en place* for the remainder of the ingredients. Spray a 9×9-inch baking dish with nonstick cooking spray. Layer the bread on the bottom of the dish. Pour half the egg mixture over the bread. Distribute the zucchini mixture over the top. Sprinkle with the Italian cheese. Top with the goat cheese and tomato. Chill, covered, until 1 hour prior to baking. Bake at 350 degrees for 35 to 40 minutes until golden brown.

Makes 6 to 8 servings

Barry Werner, Scarborough Fair Bed & Breakfast

When working with a new group of students, one of the first things I teach is the kitchen vocabulary many professionals use. Without it, it's difficult to "fit in" a commercial kitchen and even more difficult to know the right questions to ask. A great example is "mise en place" (pronounced "meez on plas"). Literally translated, it's a French phrase meaning, "putting in place." Chefs use this term to refer to assembling the ingredients needed to prepare a recipe. Fitting in is the first step to becoming a successful employee—understanding kitchen vocabulary is the first step to "fitting in." —The Chef

EGG SALAD WITH GORGONZOLA CHEESE

6 eggs, hard-cooked
3/4 cup mayonnaise
1/2 teaspoon Dijon mustard
1/8 teaspoon dry mustard
1/4 teaspoon lemon zest
1/2 tablespoon chopped fresh chives
1/8 teaspoon cayenne pepper
Salt to taste
1/2 cup crumbled Gorgonzola cheese
1 loaf rustic bread, sliced
1 head Bibb lettuce

Roughly chop the eggs. Combine the mayonnaise, Dijon mustard, dry mustard, lemon zest, chives, cayenne pepper and salt in a bowl and mix well. Add the cheese and mix lightly. Add the chopped eggs and mix lightly.

Spread the egg salad on half the bread slices. Add a leaf of lettuce to each. Top with the remaining bread to form sandwiches. Or, serve in a bowl with a garnish of red leaf lettuce and Crostini (page 91).

Makes 6 to 8 servings

Tip: For perfect hard-cooked eggs, let the eggs come to room temperature, or place them in warm water for 4 to 5 minutes before cooking. To cook, place the eggs in the water just as it starts to boil. Set a timer for 11 minutes. Cook at a low boil; drain. Roll the hot eggs in the pan to crack the shells. Cover with cold water. This method keeps the eggs from becoming tough, prevents the greenish gray sulfur ring from forming around the yolk, and allows them to be easily peeled.

Chicken a la King over Waffles

Waffles
2 cups all-purpose flour
1/4 cup bran cereal
1/2 teaspoon kosher salt
1 tablespoon sugar
4 teaspoons baking powder
1 1/2 cups (or more) milk
3 eggs
3 tablespoons butter, melted

Chicken a la King
1/2 cup chopped onion
1 cup mushrooms, sliced
1/4 cup (1/2 stick) butter
3 tablespoons all-purpose flour
1 1/2 cups chicken stock
1 cup heavy cream
1 teaspoon white pepper
1/4 teaspoon nutmeg
1 rotisserie chicken, skin removed and meat shredded
1/2 cup frozen peas

For the waffles, combine the flour, cereal, salt, sugar and baking powder in a large bowl and mix well. Whisk the milk and eggs together in a bowl. Add to the flour mixture along with the butter. Let stand for 5 minutes. If the batter becomes too thick, add additional milk. Prepare according to the waffle iron manufacturer's directions. Keep warm.

For the chicken, sauté the onion and mushrooms in the butter in a sauté pan until tender. Add the flour and cook for 1 minute. Add the stock and cook until the mixture begins to thicken, stirring constantly. Add the cream, white pepper and nutmeg. Bring to a simmer; reduce the heat and add the chicken and peas. Cook until heated through. Serve the creamed chicken over waffles.

Makes 6 servings

CRISPY YEAST WAFFLES

1 envelope dry yeast
$^1\!/2$ cup warm water
2 cups milk, warmed to
   room temperature
$^1\!/2$ cup vegetable oil

1 teaspoon salt
1 teaspoon sugar
2 cups all-purpose flour
2 eggs
$^1\!/4$ teaspoon baking soda

At least 8 hours before cooking, sprinkle the yeast over the water in a large mixing bowl. Let stand for 5 minutes. Add the milk, oil, salt, sugar and flour and whisk to blend. Cover with plastic wrap. Let stand at room temperature for 8 to 12 hours. Add the eggs and baking soda and mix well. The batter will be thin. Pour $^1\!/2$ to $^3\!/4$ cup portions of the batter onto a hot waffle iron. Cook according to the manufacturer's directions until golden brown and crisp.

Makes 6 to 8 servings

Bill Van Dyke

APPLE BACON PANCAKES

$1^1\!/2$ cups all-purpose flour
2 tablespoons sugar
2 teaspoons baking powder
1 teaspoon baking soda
1 teaspoon salt
$^1\!/4$ teaspoon cinnamon
2 eggs

$^1\!/2$ cup milk, warmed
2 Granny Smith apples, peeled and
   coarsely grated
$1^1\!/2$ pounds applewood-smoked
   bacon, crisp-cooked
   and crumbled
$^1\!/4$ cup ($^1\!/2$ stick) butter, melted

Combine the flour, sugar, baking powder, baking soda, salt and cinnamon in a large bowl and mix well. Whisk the eggs and milk in a bowl until blended. Add to the flour mixture and stir just until combined. Stir in the apples and bacon.

Heat a griddle or large heavy skillet over medium-high heat. Brush with the butter. Pour $^1\!/4$ cup portions of batter onto the hot griddle. Cook for about 2 minutes or until bubbles appear on the surface and the edges begin to brown. Turn and cook for 1 minute longer. Remove to a platter and keep warm in the oven. Serve hot with butter and maple syrup.

Makes 4 servings

Susan Bridges

GERMAN PANCAKES

One delicious way to serve this puffy pancake is with apples that have been sautéed in butter with brown sugar.

3 eggs
3/4 cup all-purpose flour
3/4 cup milk
1/2 teaspoon salt

1 1/2 tablespoons butter
2 tablespoons confectioners' sugar
1 lemon, cut into quarters

Beat the eggs, flour, milk and salt until smooth. Melt the butter in an ovenproof skillet and swirl to coat the side. Pour the batter into the hot skillet. Bake at 450 degrees for 15 minutes. Lower the temperature to 350 degrees. Bake for 10 minutes longer or until the pancake is puffed and light brown.

Divide among two or three plates. Sprinkle with the confectioners' sugar and lemon juice.

Makes 2 or 3 servings

Susan Bridges

FRENCH TOAST WITH BRIE AND CANDIED PECANS

1 loaf brioche or French bread, cut into 3/4-inch slices
4 ounces brie cheese, sliced
3 eggs
1/4 cup milk
1 teaspoon sugar

1 teaspoon Triple Sec (optional)
1/2 teaspoon vanilla extract
1 teaspoon maple syrup
1/2 cup Candied Pecans (page 180)

Cut a pocket into each bread slice. Stuff a slice of brie into each pocket. Beat the eggs in a large, shallow bowl. Add the milk, sugar, liqueur, vanilla and syrup and mix well. Soak each piece of bread in the egg mixture. Place bread on a platter after soaking. Let stand for several minutes.

Heat a large skillet. Coat with butter or nonstick cooking spray. Brown each piece of bread in the skillet. Keep warm in a warm oven. Top with the pecans. Serve with maple syrup.

Makes 4 servings

Moravian Sugar Cake

This recipe is one of many handed down from the Moravian settlers who first arrived in North Carolina in November 1753. It has been said that there is no better coffee cake in the world than a Moravian sugar cake. Moravian cooks make it throughout the year, but especially at Easter. It is a classic with many years of history.

1 large baking potato, peeled	1/4 teaspoon salt
1 envelope dry yeast	2 eggs
1/2 teaspoon sugar	31/2 cups all-purpose flour
1/4 cup warm water	1 cup light brown sugar
1/2 cup butter-flavored shortening	1 teaspoon cinnamon, or to taste
3/4 cup sugar	1/2 cup salted butter, melted

Boil the potato in water to cover in a saucepan until tender. Drain, reserving 1 cup of the cooking liquid. Mash the potato with a fork until smooth. Measure 1/2 cup of the potato; discard any unused potato.

Dissolve the yeast and 1/2 teaspoon of the sugar in the warm water in a bowl. Let stand until bubbly. Combine the reserved cooking liquid, 1/2 cup mashed potato, the shortening, 3/4 cup sugar and the salt in a bowl and mix well. Add the eggs one at a time, beating well after each addition.

Add 11/2 cups of the flour and the yeast mixture and mix well. Add 11/2 cups of the remaining flour and mix well.

Cover and let rise in a warm place for 1 to 2 hours until doubled. Stir in the remaining 1/2 cup flour. Spoon the batter into an 11×15-inch baking pan or jellyroll pan. Let rise until doubled in size.

Combine the brown sugar and cinnamon. Sprinkle over the cake. Let rise until doubled in size. Using floured fingertips, punch holes in the cake 1 to 2 inches apart. Drizzle with the melted butter. Bake at 375 degrees for 15 to 17 minutes. Serve warm or cold.

Makes 1 cake

Pat Goodyear

BLUEBERRY MUFFINS

1 cup all-purpose flour
1 cup whole wheat flour
1 tablespoon baking powder
1/4 teaspoon nutmeg
2 eggs
1/2 cup brown sugar

1/2 cup vegetable oil
1 cup heavy cream
1 1/2 teaspoons vanilla extract
1 cup pecans, toasted and chopped
1 cup blueberries, fresh or frozen

Combine the all-purpose flour, whole wheat flour, baking powder and nutmeg in a bowl; mix well. Combine the eggs, brown sugar, oil, cream and vanilla in a large mixing bowl and mix well. Add to the flour mixture. Stir for 15 to 20 seconds, just until combined. Fold in the pecans and blueberries. Divide among greased or lined muffin cups. Bake at 400 degrees for 18 to 20 minutes until golden brown.

Makes 12 muffins

Bill Van Dyke

BRAN MUFFINS

3 cups bran cereal
1 cup boiling water
1/2 cup shortening, melted
1 1/2 cups sugar
3 eggs, beaten

2 cups buttermilk
2 1/2 cups all-purpose flour
2 1/2 teaspoons baking soda
1 teaspoon salt

Combine the bran cereal and boiling water in a large bowl and mix well. Combine the shortening, sugar, eggs, buttermilk, flour, baking soda and salt in a large bowl and mix well. Add the softened bran cereal. Divide the batter among greased muffin cups. Bake at 400 degrees for 20 minutes.

Makes 36 muffins

Anne West

This excellent batter keeps in the refrigerator for up to 2 weeks, allowing you to have freshly baked muffins any time you wish.

Fresh Ginger Muffins

5 ounces fresh ginger, unpeeled
and minced
$1/4$ cup sugar
2 tablespoons lemon zest
3 tablespoons sugar
$1/2$ cup (1 stick) butter, softened

$1/2$ cup sugar
2 eggs
1 cup buttermilk
2 cups all-purpose flour
$1/2$ teaspoon salt
$3/4$ teaspoon baking soda

Cook the ginger and $1/4$ cup of the sugar in a small skillet over medium heat until the sugar is melted. Do not allow the sugar to burn. Remove from the heat.

Combine the lemon zest and 3 tablespoons sugar in a food processor. Pulse to mix. Add to the ginger mixture. Beat the butter and $1/2$ cup sugar in a bowl using an electric mixer until smooth. Beat in the eggs and buttermilk. Add the flour, salt and baking soda; mix well. Stir in the ginger mixture. Spoon into greased muffin cups. Bake at 375 degrees for 15 minutes.

Makes 12 muffins

Susan Bridges

Sour Cream Maple Muffins

$13/4$ cups all-purpose flour
2 teaspoons baking powder
1 teaspoon baking soda
$1/2$ teaspoon salt
$1/2$ cup (1 stick) unsalted butter,
softened

$3/4$ cup maple syrup
1 cup sour cream
1 egg
$1/2$ cup pecans, chopped

Combine the flour, baking powder, baking soda and salt in a small bowl. Beat the butter in a large bowl until creamy. Add the syrup gradually, beating constantly. Beat in the sour cream and egg. Stir in the pecans. Add the dry ingredients. Stir just until combined. Fill buttered muffin cups two-thirds full. Bake at 400 degrees for 15 to 18 minutes until muffins test done.

Makes 12 muffins

Susan Landry

CRANBERRY ORANGE SCONES

2¹/2 cups all-purpose flour
³/4 cup granulated sugar
1 tablespoon baking powder
³/4 teaspoon salt
1 cup (2 sticks) butter, chilled
³/4 cup dried cranberries
Zest of 1 orange

4 eggs
1 tablespoon vanilla extract
1 tablespoon orange extract
Juice of 1 orange
1 cup walnuts, chopped
1 egg white
¹/4 cup turbinado sugar

Combine the flour, granulated sugar, baking powder and salt in a bowl. Cut in the butter until the size of small peas. Add the cranberries and orange zest. Add the eggs, vanilla, orange extract, orange juice and walnuts. Mix just until the ingredients come together; do not overmix.

Form the dough into a ball. Shape into a disk about 8 inches in diameter and 2 inches thick. Arrange on a baking sheet. Beat the egg white with a small amount of water. Brush over the dough. Cut the dough into 8 equal triangles. Sprinkle with the turbinado sugar. Bake at 350 degrees for 45 minutes.

Makes 8 scones

Bill Van Dyke

Tip: Turbinado sugar is also known as raw sugar or cane sugar. It is lighter in color, and the crystals are larger and drier than those of commercial brown sugar.

Koulourakia
(Braided Greek Easter Biscuits)

1 1/2 cups (3 sticks) unsalted butter, softened
3 tablespoons vegetable oil
2/3 cup sugar
2 eggs
3 tablespoons orange juice
2 teaspoons baking powder
1 tablespoon brandy
3/4 teaspoon vanilla extract
3 3/4 cups all-purpose flour
1 egg
1 tablespoon water
2 tablespoons sesame seeds (optional)

Combine the butter, oil and sugar in a large bowl. Beat with an electric mixer for 10 minutes until light and fluffy. Add 2 eggs one at a time, beating for 5 minutes after each addition. Combine the orange juice with the baking powder in a bowl. Add to the butter mixture and mix well. And the brandy and vanilla and mix well.

Add the flour gradually, mixing by hand until the dough forms a soft, smooth ball. Let the dough rest for 15 minutes.

Cut off a golf ball-size piece of dough. Roll into a 6-inch-long rope. Fold the rope in half and twist the legs together. Form the remaining dough in the same manner.

Beat 1 egg with the water in a small bowl. Brush over the biscuits. Bake at 350 degrees for 15 minutes or until pale golden brown. Brush with the egg mixture again, then sprinkle with the sesame seeds. Bake for 5 minutes longer until golden brown.

Makes 36 biscuits

Anna Epislantis

Traditional Biscuits

2 cups all-purpose flour
1 tablespoon baking powder
3/4 teaspoon salt

3 tablespoons shortening, chilled
1 cup milk

Combine the flour, baking powder and salt in a large bowl. Cut in the shortening until the mixture resembles coarse crumbs. Make a well in the center of the mixture. Pour the milk into the well. Stir just until the dough comes together. The dough will be very sticky.

Turn the dough out onto a floured surface. Dust the top of the dough with flour. Fold gently 5 or 6 times. Roll the dough to 1 1/2 inches thick. Cut biscuits with a round cutter or a glass. Arrange on a baking sheet. Bake at 450 degrees for 12 to 15 minutes until golden brown.

Makes 12 biscuits

Betty Higman

Banana Bread

2 cups all-purpose flour
1 teaspoon baking soda
1/4 teaspoon salt
1/2 cup (1 stick) butter, softened

3/4 cup brown sugar
2 eggs, beaten
2 1/3 cups mashed very ripe
bananas

Combine the flour, baking soda and salt in a large bowl and mix well. Combine the butter and brown sugar in a medium bowl. Beat until well blended. Add the eggs and mashed bananas and mix well.

Add the banana mixture to the dry ingredients. Stir just until combined. Spoon the batter into a lightly greased loaf pan. Bake at 350 degrees for 60 minutes or until a knife inserted in the center comes out clean. Let cool for 10 minutes before slicing.

Makes 1 loaf

Karen Adkins

ZUCCHINI BREAD

3 eggs	3 cups all-purpose flour
2 cups sugar	1 teaspoon salt
1 cup vegetable oil	1 teaspoon baking soda
1 tablespoon vanilla extract	1 teaspoon baking powder
2 cups grated zucchini	1 tablespoon cinnamon

Beat the eggs in a large bowl. Add the sugar, oil, vanilla and zucchini and mix well. Combine the flour, salt, baking soda, baking powder and cinnamon in a bowl and mix well. Add to the zucchini mixture. Mix just until combined. Pour evenly into two greased 5×9-inch loaf pans. Bake at 350 degrees for 1 hour. Let cool in the pans for at least 15 minutes. Remove and cool completely.

Makes 2 loaves

Karen Adkins

CROSTINI AND CROUTONS

1 baguette
1 cup Garlic-Infused Oil (page 184)

For crostini, cut the baguette into thin rounds. Arrange on a baking sheet. Brush the infused oil on each slice. Bake at 350 degrees for 10 to 15 minutes until light brown and crisp.

For croutons, cut the baguette into bite-size cubes. Toss with the oil. Arrange in a single layer on a baking sheet. Bake at 350 degrees for 10 to 15 minutes until light brown and crisp.

Cool both crostini and croutons thoroughly before storing in an airtight container.

Makes 6 servings

Classic Corn Bread

1¹/2 cups cornmeal
1/2 cup all-purpose flour
1 tablespoon baking powder
1 teaspoon salt

2 eggs
1/4 cup vegetable oil
2 cups milk
1 tablespoon cornmeal

Combine 1¹/2 cups cornmeal, the flour, baking soda and salt in a bowl; mix well. Add the eggs, half the oil and the milk and stir just until mixed; do not overmix. Pour the remaining oil into a cast-iron skillet. Heat the skillet in a 400-degree oven until very hot. Sprinkle 1 tablespoon cornmeal into the skillet. Add the batter. Bake for 20 minutes.

Makes 8 servings

Betty Higman

Corn Bread

1/4 cup canola oil
1 cup cornmeal
1 cup all-purpose flour
1/2 teaspoon baking soda
1 tablespoon baking powder

1/2 teaspoon salt
1 tablespoon sugar
1 egg
1 cup (or more) buttermilk

Pour the canola oil into a cast-iron skillet. Heat in a 400-degree oven. Combine the cornmeal, flour, baking soda, baking powder, salt and sugar in a large bowl and mix well. Add the egg and buttermilk and mix well. The batter should be thicker than pancake batter; add more buttermilk to adjust the thickness if needed.

Pour the hot oil into the batter and mix. Pour the batter into the hot skillet. Bake for 15 minutes or until the top is brown. Cool for 5 to 10 minutes.

Makes 8 to 10 servings

Julia Van Dyke

*Tip: To substitute for buttermilk, use ¹/2 cup milk
plus ¹/2 cup yogurt for 1 cup milk. Or add 1 tablespoon vinegar to
1 cup minus 1 tablespoon milk and let stand for 5 minutes.*

HUSH PUPPIES

4 cups vegetable oil
1 cup (or more) yellow cornmeal
1/2 cup all-purpose flour
2 teaspoons baking powder
1/4 teaspoon cayenne pepper
1 teaspoon sugar
1/2 teaspoon salt

1 egg
3/4 cup milk
1/2 cup minced onion
Diced jalapeño chiles to taste
   (optional)
1 cup (4 ounces) shredded sharp
   Cheddar cheese

Heat the oil to 375 degrees in a Dutch oven. Combine the cornmeal, flour, baking powder, cayenne pepper, sugar and salt in a bowl. Beat the egg, milk, onion and jalapeño until well combined. Add to the cornmeal mixture and mix well. Stir in the cheese. The batter should be thick enough to hold its shape when dropped from a spoon. Add additional cornmeal 1 tablespoon at a time if needed for the desired consistency.

Carefully drop spoonfuls of batter into the hot oil. Do not overcrowd the Dutch oven. Cook until the hush puppies are golden brown and rise to the top. Drain on paper towels. Keep warm.

Makes 8 to 10 servings

*Hush puppies are a traditional Southern food often served
with seafood, fish, and stews.*

CARAMELIZED BACON BREADSTICKS

1/2 cup brown sugar
1/2 teaspoon cayenne pepper

12 slices bacon
12 grissini breadsticks

Combine the brown sugar and cayenne pepper in a medium bowl. Wrap the bacon around the breadsticks in a spiral pattern. Roll in the brown sugar mixture.

Cover a rimmed baking sheet with aluminum foil. Set a wire rack on the sheet. Arrange the breadsticks on the rack. Bake at 325 degrees for 15 to 20 minutes until the bacon is crisp and the sugar has caramelized.

Makes 12 breadsticks

*Life expectancy would grow by leaps and bounds if green vegetables
smelled as good as bacon.* —Doug Larson

DARK PUMPERNICKEL RYE BREAD

Bread deals with living things, with giving life, with growth,
with the seed, the grain that nurtures. It is not coincidence that we say
bread is the staff of life. —Lionel Polâne

1 envelope dry yeast
1/4 cup warm water
2 1/2 cups bread flour
1 cup medium rye flour
1 teaspoon salt
4 teaspoons baking cocoa
3/4 teaspoon onion powder
1 cup hot strong coffee
2 tablespoons vegetable oil
2 tablespoons molasses
4 teaspoons white vinegar
2 teaspoons caraway seeds
1/4 teaspoon fennel seeds

Dissolve the yeast in the warm water in a small bowl. Pour the bread flour and rye flour into the bowl of a food processor. Add the salt, baking cocoa and onion powder. Pour the coffee into a 2-cup measure. Add the oil, molasses and vinegar and mix well.

Turn on the food processor. Add the yeast mixture and coffee mixture. Process until the dough forms a ball; do not underprocess. Add the caraway seeds and fennel seeds. Pulse for 5 to 10 seconds. Place the dough in a greased bowl. Cover with plastic wrap. Let rise in a warm place for 90 minutes.

Punch down the dough. Divide it evenly between two greased 2-quart round glass baking dishes. Let rise for 90 minutes until doubled in size. Bake at 375 degrees for 25 minutes or until the loaves sound hollow when tapped on the bottom. Cool completely before slicing.

Makes 2 loaves

Pat Goodyear

BUTTERHORN ROLLS

1¹/4 cups milk
2 envelopes dry yeast
1 teaspoon sugar
¹/2 cup (1 stick) butter

¹/2 cup sugar
3 eggs, beaten
1 teaspoon salt
4 to 5 cups all-purpose flour

Heat ¹/4 cup of the milk to lukewarm, about 100 degrees. Dissolve the yeast and 1 teaspoon sugar in the lukewarm milk in a small bowl.

Heat the remaining 1 cup milk to very warm. Combine the butter and ¹/2 cup sugar in a bowl. Pour the warm milk over the top. Add the eggs, salt and 2 cups of the flour. Add the yeast mixture and mix well. Let rise in a warm place until the dough is doubled in size.

Add 2 more cups of the flour. Knead the dough for several minutes, adding more flour as needed to create a dough that is soft but not sticky.

Pinch off 1-inch pieces of dough. Place three pieces in each muffin cup (for a cloverleaf roll). Let rise until almost doubled. Bake at 350 degrees for 20 to 25 minutes until golden brown.

Makes 36 rolls

FRESH TOMATO PIZZA

4 garlic cloves, minced
1 teaspoon olive oil
1 loaf frozen bread dough, thawed
6 large tomatoes, sliced
White pepper to taste

4 or 5 slices provolone cheese
¹/2 cup (2 ounces) shredded
   part-skim mozzarella cheese
10 to 12 fresh basil leaves

Sauté the garlic in the olive oil in a skillet. Roll the dough on a floured surface to the desired shape and pan size. Fit in a baking pan or on a pizza stone. Spread the garlic oil over the dough. Bake at 425 degrees for 5 minutes. Maintain the oven temperature.

Arrange the tomatoes over the dough. Season with white pepper. Cover the tomatoes with the provolone cheese. Sprinkle mozzarella over the provolone. Top with the basil leaves. Bake for 15 to 20 minutes until the cheese melts and the crust is golden brown. Let stand to cool for several minutes before serving.

Makes 6 servings

Karen Adkins

FLATBREAD

12 cups all-purpose flour
1 tablespoon dry yeast
1 teaspoon salt
2 tablespoons dried thyme
2 tablespoons dried rosemary
3/4 cup plus 2 tablespoons olive oil
2 to 3 cups water

Combine the flour, yeast, salt, thyme and rosemary in a mixer fitted with a dough hook. Add the olive oil and 2 cups water and mix until the dough has a sticky consistency, adding additional water as needed. Separate the dough into 5-ounce pieces (about 20). Cover with a clean kitchen towel. Let rise until doubled in size.

Punch down the dough balls. Shape into flat rounds and arrange on a baking sheet. Bake at 400 degrees for 7 to 8 minutes until golden brown.

Makes about 20 servings

Chef Manolo Acin, The Harbor Court Hotel

Variation: *For suggestions to make a smaller amount or for a Goat Cheese Ricotta Topping suggestion, see page 16.*

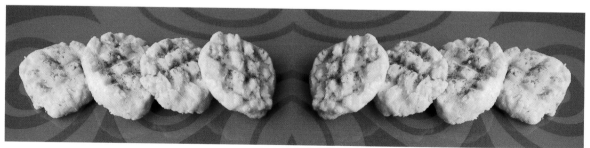

104

COLOR PHOTOGRAPH DESCRIPTION

Page	Photo Description	Name of Recipe
Page 97	Cold Soup Linguine	Crème Baltimore Spicy Shrimp and Linguine
Page 98	Grilled Caesar Prep	Grilled Caesar Salad
Page 99	Grilled Tuna Prep	Tuna Fillets with Tamarind Rum Sauce
Page 100–101	Centerfold of Chicken	Mosaic Grilled Chicken with Vegetables
Page 102	Eggplant Sandwich and Shortbreads	Grilled Eggplant and Muenster on Ciabatta Sharp Cheese and Pecan Shortbread
Page 103	Salmon Rolls	Grilled Salmon Wraps with Strawberry Jalapeño Barbecue Sauce
Page 104	Eggplant Napoleon	Eggplant Napoleon
Page 105	Cheesecake	Savory Cheesecake with Polenta Crust
Page 106	Meatballs Mac' and Cheese Soup Risotto	Cocktail Meatballs with Strawberry Jalapeño Sauce Shrimp Mac' and Cheese Black Bean Soup Risotto with Trio of Mushrooms
Page 107	Working hands	
Page 108	Asian Spoon Pork with Marmalade Salmon with chutney	Watermelon and Blue Cheese Salad Red Onion and Bacon Marmalade Cedar-Planked Salmon, Tomato Mango Chutney
Page 109	Chicken bite with fork Asian Spoon Lobster	Almond-Encrusted Chicken Bites with Zesty Dipping Sauce Lobster Spoons
Page 110–111	Centerfold of Pies	Chocolate Pie, Coconut Cream Pie, Cherry Pie, Lemon Meringue Pie, Butterscotch Pie, Pie Crust
Page 112	Culinary Students & Instructor	

113

Tim Kelly

"When you lose your housing, your children ask every day, 'When are we going home Mom? I want to go home. Why can't we go home?' When you tell them there is nothing mommy can do to get a home right now, a look of disappointment comes over their faces and sketches itself into your memory forever. Then one day, you say, 'Guess what kids? We're going home today!' The kids are awestruck, scared to believe it; they don't react. After a while they realize it's true—they're not going back to the shelter! Now they can trust again that you are able to scare big, bad monsters from under their beds and leap tall buildings. All is right with their world, with your family when you have a home. I am so grateful for everyone who helped me provide a home for my family."

Susan

Former resident, graduate of supportive housing program

SUPPORTIVE HOUSING:
A NEW HOME, A NEW BEGINNING

The goal of supportive housing is to be an interim step between the emergency shelter and market housing. Residents from the emergency shelter who are working full-time are moved to supportive housing. During the two years they reside in supportive housing, goals are set for each family and often include repairing credit histories, finding a better job (full-time with benefits making a living wage), and dealing with the issues that resulted in homelessness.

Most of the women in our program make between $8.00 and $11.00 an hour. Our homes rent for $500 a month—below market value for the Baltimore area. In Baltimore City, decent, affordable housing is hard to find. In the past five years, BOS has focused on expanding the number of supportive housing units we can provide so that families have a home of their own. BOS currently has nine houses—two that we rent and seven that we own.

Homes are completely furnished with all the basics that a family needs—dishes, pots and pans, beds, dressers, mattresses, linens, dining room furniture, and living furniture. Most of these furnishings are donated. When women complete their program, all of the household furnishings are theirs to take with them.

Sixteen women have completed two years in supportive housing and are successfully working, supporting their families, and living in market-rate housing. Three women eventually became homeowners after completing the supportive housing program.

DINNER WITH A TWIST

Menu

Flatbread with Goat Cheese Ricotta

*Mixed Field Greens with Creamy Avocado Dressing
and Croutons*

Short Ribs Sabatelli

Creamy Cheese Polenta with Gorgonzola Cream Cheese Sauce

Grilled Asparagus

Fruit Cobbler with vanilla ice cream

*Sometimes the menu calls for meat and potatoes.
Other times, try something different by replacing potatoes with creamy
polenta. The hearty eaters on your list will love this meal!*

Beef Tenderloin with Dijon Horseradish Sauce

4 pounds beef tenderloin
2 tablespoons Dijon mustard
1 tablespoon molasses
2 tablespoons garlic pepper

1 teaspoon kosher salt
Dijon Horseradish Sauce
(recipe below)

Trim the tenderloin and remove the chain (the strip of excess meat that runs the length of the tenderloin.) Fold the thinner tip of the meat under and tie with butcher's string.

Combine the Dijon mustard and molasses. Coat the tenderloin with the mustard mixture. Combine the garlic pepper and kosher salt. Sprinkle all over the tenderloin.

Sear the tenderloin on a hot grill for 15 minutes or until brown and crusty. Move away from the heat. Close the grill and cook over indirect heat for 20 to 25 minutes for rare to medium-rare. Let stand for 10 to 15 minutes before slicing. Serve with horseradish sauce.

Makes 8 to 10 servings

To prepare the tenderloin without a grill, sear the tenderloin in a small amount of oil in a hot skillet until brown and crusty all over. Place in a roasting pan. Roast at 350 degrees for 20 to 25 minutes.

Dijon Horseradish Sauce

1 cup sour cream
1/2 cup mayonnaise
1/2 cup Dijon mustard
1 tablespoon prepared horseradish

1/2 teaspoon white pepper
Dash of Tabasco sauce
Dash of Worcestershire sauce

Combine the sour cream, mayonnaise, Dijon mustard, horseradish, white pepper, Tabasco sauce and Worcestershire sauce in a bowl and mix well. The sauce may be prepared in advance and refrigerated. Let stand for about 1 hour at room temperature before serving.

Makes 2 cups

Pepper Steak

1 (1-pound) flank steak
1/4 cup soy sauce, or to taste
1 tablespoon sherry
1 tablespoon cornstarch
1 teaspoon sugar
1/4 cup vegetable oil
2 green bell peppers, sliced
1 tomato, cut into wedges
1 slice fresh ginger (or to taste), or 1/8 teaspoon dried ground ginger
3 green onions, sliced on the diagonal
Hot cooked rice

Freeze the steak for 30 minutes to help in cutting thin slices. Cut across the grain into slices about 1/8 inch thick and 2 inches long. Combine with the soy sauce, sherry, cornstarch and sugar in a bowl. Heat 2 tablespoons of the oil in a skillet just until it begins to smoke. Stir-fry the bell peppers in the oil for 1 minute until they turn bright green. Add the tomatoes and cook briefly. Remove the bell peppers and tomatoes from the skillet.

Add the remaining 2 tablespoons oil and the ginger to the skillet. Add the steak and green onions. Cook for 2 to 3 minutes until the steak is almost cooked through, turning constantly. Add the bell peppers and tomatoes and heat through. Add more soy sauce, sherry or water if needed. Spoon onto a platter. Serve over hot cooked rice.

Makes 4 servings

Mary Graul

POT ROAST

3 onions, sliced
$1/2$ tablespoon vegetable oil
4 pounds beef bottom round
1 tablespoon vinegar
$1/4$ cup ketchup
1 cup hot water
4 or 5 whole cloves
2 or 3 bay leaves
Salt and pepper to taste
2 tablespoons all-purpose flour, or as needed

Brown the onions in the oil in a Dutch oven or enameled cast-iron casserole. Remove the onions from the skillet using a slotted spoon. Add the beef to the Dutch oven and brown on both sides; drain the oil.

Return the beef and onions to the pan. Add the vinegar, ketchup and water. Add the cloves and bay leaves. Cover and simmer for 45 minutes per pound until the beef is fork-tender, turning halfway through the cooking process.

Remove the beef from the pan. Let stand for 30 minutes. Discard the bay leaves.

Combine the cooking liquid and the flour and mix well. Cook until thickened, stirring constantly. Cut the beef into slices and return to the Dutch oven. Cook over low heat for 15 minutes. Keep warm but do not cook further.

Makes 6 servings

Jane Sabatelli

BEEF BRISKET

1 teaspoon kosher salt	3 tablespoons olive oil
2 tablespoons garlic pepper	3 carrots, cubed
1 (6- to 7-pound) beef brisket, trimmed	1 onion, cut into wedges
	2 ribs celery, chopped
2 tablespoons flour	2 cups beef broth

Combine the salt and garlic pepper in a small bowl. Sprinkle over all sides of the brisket. Dust lightly with the flour.

Brown the brisket on all sides in the olive oil in a roasting pan. Add the carrots, onion and celery and stir to coat with oil. Add the broth. Cover with a tight-fitting lid or aluminum foil.

Roast at 400 degrees for 30 minutes. Lower the heat to 350 degrees and roast for 3 hours longer. Remove from the oven and let stand, covered, for 30 minutes. Pour the pan liquid (au jus) into a gravy boat. Cut the brisket into slices and arrange on a serving platter. Surround with the vegetables. Serve with au jus.

Makes 4 to 6 servings

SHORT RIBS SABATELLI

*This was Pastor Sabatelli's prize-winning recipe for
Diakon's Katherine's Kloset fund-raiser.*

5 pounds beef short ribs	2/3 cup ketchup
1/2 tablespoon olive oil	1/4 cup soy sauce
1 onion, sliced	3 tablespoons honey
1 1/2 cups red wine	

Brown the ribs in the olive oil in a skillet or Dutch oven. Add the onion, wine, ketchup, soy sauce and honey and mix well. Simmer for 2 to 3 hours until tender. Skim any fat from the surface before serving.

Makes 6 servings

John Sabatelli

CLIPPER CITY BRAISED SHORT RIBS

8 pounds boneless short ribs
Salt and pepper to taste
2 tablespoons canola oil
2 onions, chopped
2 carrots, chopped
3 ribs celery, chopped
2 tablespoons canola oil

2 tablespoons tomato paste
1 garlic clove, chopped
3 bay leaves
2 (12-ounce) bottles Clipper City
    beer or other pale ale
Sweet Potato Hash (recipe below)
Onion Rings (recipe below)

Season the ribs all over with salt and pepper. Sear on both sides in 2 tablespoons canola oil in a skillet. Remove from the pan. Sauté the onions, carrots and celery in 2 tablespoons canola oil in the skillet. Add the tomato paste, garlic and bay leaves. Add the beer and mix well. Return the ribs to the pan. Add water to cover. Simmer for 1 hour or until the ribs are tender. Serve on a bed of Sweet Potato Hash. Top with Onion Rings.

SWEET POTATO HASH

12 sweet potatoes, peeled
    and diced
Leaves of 1 bunch rosemary, chopped

Leaves of 1 bunch thyme, chopped
3/4 cup honey
2 tablespoons olive oil

Steam the sweet potatoes until tender. Sauté the sweet potatoes, rosemary, thyme and honey in the olive oil until golden brown.

ONION RINGS

1 onion, sliced
2 cups all-purpose flour

1 teaspoon Old Bay Seasoning
1 cup vegetable oil

Separate the onion into rings. Combine the flour with the Old Bay seasoning in a shallow dish. Coat the onions with the flour mixture. Fry in the hot oil in a deep skillet until crisp.

Makes 8 to 10 servings

Chef Edwin "Zeus" Harmon, Harbor Court Hotel

SHEPHERD'S PIE

FILLING
$1/2$ teaspoon minced garlic
1 cup diced onion
$1/2$ cup diced celery
$1/2$ cup diced carrots
$1/2$ cup diced green beans
2 tablespoons olive oil
1 pound lean ground beef
1 (14-ounce) can fire-roasted tomatoes
$1/2$ teaspoon salt
$1/2$ teaspoon garlic pepper
$1/2$ teaspoon chipotle chili powder
1 tablespoon chopped parsley

TOPPING
6 large russet potatoes, peeled and cubed
1 cup (2 sticks) butter, softened
12 ounces cream cheese, softened
$1/4$ cup milk
$1/2$ teaspoon salt
$1/2$ teaspoon pepper
$3/4$ cup (3 ounces) shredded sharp Cheddar cheese

For the filling, sauté the garlic, onion, celery, carrots and green beans in the olive oil in a skillet. Add the beef. Cook until the vegetables are tender and the beef is brown and crumbly, stirring frequently; drain. Add the tomatoes, salt, garlic pepper, chili powder and parsley and mix well. Spoon the filling into a 9×9-inch baking dish.

For the topping, cook the potatoes in boiling salted water in a saucepan until tender. Drain, reserving $3/4$ cup of the cooking water. Pour the water over the filling.

Whip or mash the potatoes with the butter, cream cheese, milk, salt and pepper until smooth and well blended. The potatoes should be stiff enough to hold a peak; too much butter will cause the potatoes to flatten during baking.

Spread the potato topping over the ground beef as if frosting a cake. Sprinkle with the Cheddar cheese. Bake at 350 degrees for 30 minutes.

Makes 6 to 8 servings

Italian Meatballs

Marinara Sauce
1 onion, minced
2 tablespoons olive oil
3 cups tomato paste
3$1/2$ cups tomato sauce

Meatballs
1$1/2$ pounds ground beef
1$1/2$ pounds ground pork
1 cup Romano cheese
1$1/4$ cups fine bread crumbs
$1/2$ cup minced parsley
1 cup minced celery
4 eggs
4 garlic cloves, minced
1 teaspoon salt
$1/4$ teaspoon pepper
Vegetable oil
Hot cooked pasta

For the marinara sauce, sauté the onion in the olive oil in a large saucepan until translucent. Add the tomato paste and tomato sauce and mix well. Simmer until hot.

For the meatballs, combine the beef, pork, cheese, bread crumbs, parsley, celery, eggs, garlic, salt and pepper in a large bowl and mix well. Form into golfball-size meatballs. Brown in oil in a sauté pan in batches; drain.

Add the meatballs to the sauce. Cook over low heat for 1$1/2$ hours, adding water to sauce as needed so meatballs are covered while cooking. Serve over hot cooked pasta.

Makes 6 to 8 servings

Betty Higman

Not bad for homemade —Betty Higman

Veal Osso Buco

*Osso buco is Italian for "bone with a hole," referring to the
marrow hole in the center of a cross-cut veal shank. An experienced
butcher will know exactly how to cut the veal shank into
the medallions necessary for this flavorful stew.*

4 cross-cut veal shanks
$1/2$ cup all-purpose flour
$1/2$ teaspoon kosher salt
$1/2$ teaspoon pepper
$1/4$ cup vegetable oil
1 cup chopped onion
1 cup diagonally sliced carrots
$1/2$ cup diagonally sliced celery
2 garlic cloves, diced
$1/2$ cup sliced mushrooms
1 tablespoon all-purpose flour
2 cups dry white wine
1 cup beef broth
1 (8-ounce) can tomato sauce
$1/2$ teaspoon chopped fresh thyme leaves
2 bay leaves
Hot cooked Saffron Rice (page 168)

Coat the veal with a mixture of $1/2$ cup flour, the salt and pepper. Brown in the oil in a deep ovenproof 10-inch skillet. Remove from the skillet with a slotted spoon. Add the onion, carrots, celery and garlic and sauté until the onion is translucent. Stir in the mushrooms and sauté briefly. Add 1 tablespoon flour to the skillet and mix well. Add the wine, broth and tomato sauce and mix well. Add the thyme and bay leaves. Return the veal to the skillet; cover.

Bake at 350 degrees for 1 hour. Let stand, covered, for 15 minutes. Discard the bay leaves. Serve over saffron rice or risotto.

Makes 4 servings

MARINATED LEG OF LAMB

7^1/2 pounds leg of lamb
2 garlic cloves
3/4 cup dry red wine
1/2 cup olive oil
2 tablespoons fresh lemon juice
2 tablespoons minced parsley
1 teaspoon dried oregano
1/2 teaspoon salt
3 bay leaves
2 white onions, thinly sliced

Cut 16 slits at regular intervals along each side of the lamb. Cut each garlic clove into 8 slivers. Insert a sliver of garlic into each slit. Arrange the lamb in a ceramic or glass dish.

Combine the wine, olive oil, lemon juice, parsley, oregano, salt, bay leaves and onions in a bowl. Pour over the lamb. Cover with plastic wrap. Chill in the refrigerator for up to 2 days, turning and basting every 12 hours.

Drain the lamb, reserving the marinade. Bring the lamb to room temperature. Grill over a hot grill for 15 to 20 minutes on each side for rare, basting frequently with the marinade.

Makes 6 to 8 servings

Kay Wohlson

Tip: A leg of lamb will range from seven to ten pounds on average. When determining the number of servings, allow 2^1/2 to 3 pounds for the weight of the bone. Always let roasted meat rest before carving. Serve lamb with classic mint jelly or spice it up with chutney.

CURRIED LAMB TAGINE

2 tablespoons all-purpose flour
$1/8$ teaspoon cinnamon
$1/2$ teaspoon madras curry powder, or to taste
2 pounds lamb, cut into 1-inch cubes
$1/4$ cup olive oil
1 cup chopped onion
1 garlic clove, minced
1 cup diced carrots
1 cup diced celery
2 cups beef broth
1 cup currants
$1/2$ cup kalamata olives, pitted
Couscous with Dried Apricots (recipe below)

Combine the flour, cinnamon and curry powder in a large bowl. Add the lamb and toss to coat. Brown the lamb in the olive oil in a roasting pan. Add the onion, garlic, carrots and celery and cook 3 to 5 minutes longer. Add the broth, currants and olives.

Bake, covered, at 350 degrees for 45 minutes. Let stand for 10 minutes, then uncover. Serve over Couscous with Dried Apricots.

Makes 6 servings

COUSCOUS WITH DRIED APRICOTS

2 cups chicken stock
2 tablespoons extra-virgin olive oil
1 cup couscous
$1/2$ cup dried apricots, coarsely chopped
$1/4$ cup coarsely chopped fresh mint

Bring the stock and olive oil to a boil in a saucepan. Add the couscous and apricots. Remove from the heat and cover. Let stand for 5 minutes or until all the liquid has been absorbed. Fluff with a fork and add the mint to serve.

Pozole (Pork and Hominy Stew)

1 pound dried hominy
1 tablespoon chopped cilantro
1 teaspoon fresh oregano, chopped
1 teaspoon dried marjoram
1 teaspoon dried thyme
1 teaspoon chili powder
1/2 teaspoon salt
1 teaspoon pepper
2 pounds pork shoulder or
   pork roast, cubed
1 cup chopped white onion
2 tablespoons minced garlic
1 tablespoon olive oil
8 cups (or more) chicken stock

Salt to taste
2 pounds fresh tomatillos,
   husks removed
4 dried ancho chiles, seeded,
   deveined and soaked in hot
   water to soften
1 (4-ounce) can diced green chiles,
   or more to taste
1 avocado, diced
Chopped cilantro
10 warm corn tortillas
2 fresh jalapeño chiles, chopped
3 limes, cut into wedges
1 small bag pork rinds

Soak the hominy in water for at least 8 hours. Combine 1 tablespoon cilantro, the oregano, marjoram, thyme, chili powder, 1/2 teaspoon salt and the pepper in a bowl. Reserve some of the rub to season the stew. Rub the remaining rub over the pork. Let stand for 1 hour. Sauté the onion and garlic in the olive oil in a large pot. Add the pork and brown all over. Add the stock. Cook, tightly covered, over low heat for 2 to 2 1/2 hours until the pork is tender.

Bring a pot of heavily salted water to a boil. Add the tomatillos. Cook for 10 minutes; drain. Drain the ancho chiles. Purée the tomatillos, ancho chiles and green chiles in a blender or food processor. Remove the pork from the cooking liquid. Add the hominy to the liquid. Cook for 30 minutes or until tender. If the liquid becomes too thick, add more stock.

Add the pork and tomatillo mixture to the pan. Simmer over low heat for 1 hour. Season with the reserved rub mixture. Serve the stew in deep bowls. Top evenly with the avocado, cilantro, tortillas, jalapeños, lime wedges and pork rinds.

Makes 10 servings

Lesley Miller

In an "authentic" Mexican home, guajillo and cascabel chiles would be used in addition to the chiles normally found in the United States. Like the ancho chile in the stew, they are seeded, deveined, and soaked in hot water until softened.

PORK TENDERLOIN WITH MUSHROOM WINE SAUCE

1 (1-pound) pork tenderloin
2 teaspoons garlic pepper
1/2 teaspoon kosher salt
1/4 cup olive oil
1 tablespoon minced shallot
2 1/2 cups baby portobello mushrooms, stemmed and sliced
1 cup dry white wine
1 1/2 cups chicken stock

Season the pork with the garlic pepper and salt. Sear the pork in 2 tablespoons of the olive oil in a large ovenproof skillet. Remove to a platter and keep warm.

Heat the remaining 2 tablespoons olive oil in the skillet. Add the shallot and mushrooms and sauté until tender. Add the wine. Simmer for 1 minute. Add the stock. Return the pork to the skillet.

Cover the skillet with a lid or foil. Braise in a 350-degree oven for 25 to 30 minutes until the internal temperature of the pork registers 145 degrees. Let stand for 10 minutes before slicing.

Bring the pan juices and mushrooms to a boil. Spoon over the pork to serve.

Makes 4 servings

SPRING PORK TENDERLOIN

2 pounds pork tenderloins, cut into $1/2$-inch medallions
2 tablespoons hoisin sauce
Sesame oil
$1/4$ green bell pepper, julienned
$1/4$ red bell pepper, julienned
$1/4$ yellow bell pepper, julienned
$1/4$ orange bell pepper, julienned
$1/4$ Vidalia onion, julienned
$1/2$ cup sweet Thai chili sauce
2 tablespoons heavy cream
Saffron Rice (page 168)
Toasted sesame seeds

Combine the pork and hoisin sauce in a bowl. Sauté the pork in sesame oil in a large skillet. Add the bell peppers, onion, chili sauce and cream. Simmer for 10 to 15 minutes until the vegetables are tender-crisp and the sauce has thickened. Serve over Saffron Rice sprinkled with sesame seeds.

Makes 6 servings

Bruce Dorsey, Metropolitan Café

APRICOT CHICKEN

1 onion, minced
1/2 teaspoon chopped garlic
2 tablespoons olive oil
2 cups orange marmalade
2 cups apricot preserves
1/2 teaspoon salt
White pepper to taste
1 cup chicken stock
Zest and sections of 1 orange
1 tablespoon cornstarch
1/3 cup cold water
1 tablespoon minced parsley
6 chicken breasts, grilled

Sauté the onion and garlic in the olive oil in a heavy saucepan until translucent. Add the marmalade, preserves, salt, white pepper, stock, orange zest and orange sections and mix well. Bring to a boil.

Combine the cornstarch and water in a small bowl and mix well. Add to the marmalade mixture. Cook until the mixture thickens, stirring constantly. Let cool.

Pour the sauce through a strainer. Add the parsley. Reheat the sauce. Serve over the chicken.

Makes 6 servings

Tip: An important food safety practice is avoiding cross-contamination. Use color-coded cutting boards or flex mats when preparing raw poultry or other meat. When finished with the board, be sure to wash it with hot soapy water to sanitize it properly. Use a different color board for all other food preparation.

BRICK OVEN CHICKEN WITH MUSTARD CREAM SAUCE

6 boneless chicken breasts
2 tablespoons olive oil
1 garlic clove, minced
2 teaspoons white pepper
1 teaspoon kosher salt

1 teaspoon paprika
1/2 teaspoon poultry seasoning
Mustard Cream Sauce
  (recipe below)

Wrap three clean masonry bricks with foil. Place the bricks in the oven. Preheat to 350 degrees.

Coat the chicken with the olive oil. Combine the garlic, white pepper, salt, paprika and poultry seasoning in a shallow dish. Coat the chicken with the seasoning mixture.

Pull the skin evenly over the meat of the chicken breast. Arrange the chicken pieces skin side down very close together in a cast-iron skillet. Pull any loose edges of skin around the back (up side) of each chicken breast.

Remove the hot bricks from the oven. Place on top of the chicken. Put the skillet in the oven. Bake for 20 to 30 minutes until the chicken registers 165 degrees and the juices run clear. Remove the bricks from the chicken. Top each chicken breast with a dollop of Mustard Cream Sauce to serve.

Makes 6 servings

Tip: *Select chicken breasts that are about the same size to ensure equal cooking time.*

MUSTARD CREAM SAUCE

1 pint (2 cups) heavy cream
2 tablespoons Dijon mustard
1/4 teaspoon cayenne pepper

1/4 teaspoon dry mustard
1/4 teaspoon nutmeg

Chill a mixing bowl and beaters in the freezer for 20 minutes. Whip the cream, Dijon mustard, cayenne pepper, dry mustard and nutmeg in the chilled bowl until the cream holds a peak. Refrigerate.

Makes about 2 cups

CHIANTI-GLAZED CHICKEN WITH KALAMATA OLIVES

8 chicken tenderloins
Salt and pepper to taste
1 tablespoon all-purpose flour
1 tablespoon olive oil
1 garlic clove, minced
1 shallot, minced
1 cup chianti

1 teaspoon orange marmalade
1/2 tablespoon balsamic vinegar
1 teaspoon capers
2 teaspoons roughly chopped
  kalamata olives
Creamy Cheese Polenta (page 165)

Season the chicken with salt and pepper. Dust with the flour. Brown the chicken in the olive oil in a skillet for 2 to 3 minutes. Remove from the skillet.

Sauté the garlic and shallots in the drippings in the skillet for 1 minute. Add the wine, marmalade and vinegar. Simmer until reduced by about half. Add the capers and olives. Serve with Creamy Cheese Polenta.

Makes 4 servings

OVEN-FRIED CHICKEN

1 teaspoon kosher salt
1 tablespoon garlic pepper
1 teaspoon chipotle chili powder
1 teaspoon poultry seasoning

4 skin-on bone-in chicken breasts
4 skin-on bone-in chicken thighs
3/4 cup all-purpose flour

Combine the salt, garlic pepper, chili powder and poultry seasoning in a small bowl. Use some of the seasoning mixture to season the chicken pieces.

Combine the remaining seasoning mixture with the flour in a large paper or plastic bag. Add the chicken and shake the bag to coat. Shake any excess coating from the chicken. Pull chicken skin over any exposed meat.

Spray a large cast-iron skillet with nonstick cooking spray. Arrange the chicken thighs in the center of the skillet. Arrange the chicken breasts around the thighs. Spray the chicken with nonstick cooking spray to ensure a crispy crust. Bake at 400 degrees for 15 minutes. Reduce the oven temperature to 350 degrees and bake for 40 minutes longer or until the chicken is golden brown and crisp and registers 165 on a meat thermometer.

Makes 6 servings

Drunken Chicken

4 boneless chicken breasts
2 tablespoons soy sauce
2 egg yolks
1/2 to 3/4 cup cornstarch
5 tablespoons olive oil
1/4 cup vodka
2 garlic cloves, thinly sliced
1 pound white button mushrooms, sliced
3 plum tomatoes, seeded and diced
3 green onions, sliced
Kosher salt and pepper to taste
1 tablespoon fresh tarragon, or 1 1/2 teaspoons dried tarragon

Pound the chicken between two pieces of plastic wrap to an even thickness. Combine with the soy sauce in a bowl. Let stand 10 minutes.

Beat the egg yolks in a shallow bowl. Place the cornstarch in another shallow bowl. Dip the chicken into the egg yolk, then coat with the cornstarch.

Sauté the chicken in the olive oil in a skillet for 3 to 4 minutes on each side until cooked through. Remove from the skillet and keep warm. Add the vodka and garlic to the skillet. Bring to a boil and boil for 1 minute. Add the mushrooms, tomatoes and green onions. Cook over high heat until the mushrooms are tender. Season with salt and pepper. Return the chicken to the pan. Cook until heated through.

Remove the pan from the heat. Add the tarragon. Arrange the chicken on a warmed serving platter. Top with the sauce.

Makes 4 servings

Pat Goodyear

MOSAIC GRILLED CHICKEN WITH VEGETABLES

*This recipe is a festive one-dish presentation with something
for everyone. It includes various fresh, marinated, and grilled vegetables
and chicken presented in a mosaic design on a large serving
platter bursting with color and flavor. The recipe has many steps,
but is well worth the time and effort!*

CHICKEN
3 boneless skinless chicken breasts
1 tablespoon olive oil
Salt and pepper to taste

VEGETABLES
8 ounces asparagus, trimmed
8 ounces baby green beans, trimmed
1 1/2 pounds fingerling potatoes
1 onion, cut into wedges
3/4 cup Garlic-Infused Oil (page 184)
1/2 red bell pepper, cut into strips
1/2 yellow bell pepper, cut into strips

For the chicken, coat the chicken with the olive oil. Season with salt and pepper. Grill over medium heat to 165 degrees on a meat thermometer. Remove the chicken to a bowl. Let stand, tightly covered with foil, for 30 minutes. Cut into strips. Return the chicken and its juices to the bowl.

For the vegetables, bring a pan of water to a rolling boil. Add the asparagus and cook for 1 minute. Plunge into ice water to stop the cooking process. Prepare the green beans in the same manner. Drain the asparagus and green beans on paper towels.

Cut the potatoes into halves lengthwise, placing the cut potatoes in a bowl of cold water; drain and pat dry. Combine the potatoes, onion and infused oil in a bowl and toss to coat. Remove the potatoes and onion with a slotted spoon to a foil-lined baking sheet. Roast at 350 degrees until brown and tender. Season with salt and pepper. Heat a dry skillet over high heat. Add the bell peppers. Sear until lightly charred but still crisp. Let cool.

5 cups mixed field greens
1 (7-ounce) jar marinated mushrooms
1 (7-ounce) jar marinated artichoke hearts
1 1/2 cups grape tomatoes, halved
1 1/2 cups mozzarella balls
1/2 cup kalamata olives, pitted (optional)
Balsamic Dressing (recipe below)

To assemble, arrange the field greens around the rim of a large serving platter. Arrange the chicken, asparagus, green beans, potatoes, onion, bell peppers, mushrooms, artichokes, tomatoes and mozzarella in rows by color to create a mosaic design. Top with the olives. Drizzle with the dressing.

Makes 6 to 8 servings

BALSAMIC DRESSING

1/4 cup balsamic vinegar
1 teaspoon Dijon mustard
2 garlic cloves, roasted and minced
1/4 teaspoon pepper
Salt to taste
1 1/4 cups light olive oil

Combine the vinegar, Dijon mustard, garlic, pepper and salt in a bowl. Whisk in the olive oil gradually until well combined.

Makes 6 to 8 servings

It is so beautifully arranged on the plate, you know someone's fingers have been all over it. —Julia Child

Rosemary Grilled Chicken with Tomato Mango Chutney

Tomato Mango Chutney
2 cups diced white onions
4 garlic cloves, minced
1 tablespoon olive oil
1 (28-ounce) can petite-
  diced tomatoes
1 cup golden raisins,
  roughly chopped
1 (8-ounce) jar hot or mild
  mango chutney
1 tablespoon balsamic vinegar
1 tablespoon mustard seeds
1 teaspoon red pepper flakes
1 teaspoon garlic pepper

Grilled Chicken
6 boneless skinless chicken breasts
1 tablespoon olive oil
1 teaspoon coarsely ground pepper
1 teaspoon fresh rosemary leaves,
  chopped
$1/2$ teaspoon poultry seasoning
$1/2$ teaspoon garlic powder
$1/2$ teaspoon kosher salt

For the chutney, sauté the onions and garlic in the olive oil in a saucepan until the onions are translucent. Add the tomatoes. Lower the heat and simmer until the liquid is reduced by half. Add the raisins, chutney, vinegar, mustard seeds, pepper flakes and garlic pepper. Simmer until the mixture is thick and jamlike. (The chutney can be made in advance and stored in airtight containers in the refrigerator for several weeks. Bring to room temperature or heat in the microwave to use.)

For the chicken, wash the chicken and pat dry. Combine the chicken and olive oil in a bowl and toss to coat. Combine the pepper, rosemary, poultry seasoning, garlic powder and salt in a small bowl and mix well. Season the chicken on both sides with the seasoning mixture. Grill over medium heat with the grill cover closed until the chicken registers 165 degrees on a meat thermometer. Remove the chicken to a clean container. Cover tightly. Let stand 10 to 15 minutes. Cut into slices and fan on a plate. Top with Tomato Mango Chutney.

Makes 6 servings

Tip: *Allowing the chicken to rest, covered, will make it more moist and easier to slice. Be sure to pour any accumulated juices over the sliced chicken.*

Chicken with Raspberry Cream Sauce

4 boneless skinless chicken breasts
1/2 teaspoon kosher salt
1/2 teaspoon white pepper
2 tablespoons olive oil
1/4 cup diagonally sliced baby leeks (white portion only)
1/2 cup white wine
3/4 cup chicken broth
1/2 cup heavy cream
1 tablespoon chopped tarragon
1 cup raspberries

Season the chicken with the salt and white pepper. Sauté in the olive oil in a skillet until brown on both sides and a meat thermometer registers 165 degrees. Remove from the skillet and keep warm.

Add the leeks to the skillet. Cook for several minutes until tender. Add the wine, broth and cream. Simmer until the sauce begins to thicken. Return the chicken and any accumulated juices to the skillet. Add the tarragon. Cook for several minutes. Turn off the heat. Add the raspberries to the sauce and stir gently to coat.

Arrange the chicken on a warm platter. Top each piece of chicken with the sauce.

Makes 4 servings

Tip: A bias- or angled-cut vegetable exposes more surface, allowing a more attractive presentation. This type of cut can be achieved by holding your knife at an angle while slicing.

CHICKEN VERONIQUE

8 boneless chicken breasts, cut into halves
1/2 cup (1 stick) butter, melted
Garlic salt to taste
White pepper to taste
1/2 cup all-purpose flour
1/2 cup (1 stick) butter, melted
3 cups chicken broth, heated
1 cup white wine
Salt to taste
2 cups sour cream, at room temperature
2 cups seedless green grapes

Brush the chicken with 1/2 cup butter. Season with garlic salt and white pepper. Roast the chicken skin side up in a ceramic dish at 450 degrees until golden brown and the chicken registers 165 degrees on a meat thermometer.

Stir the flour into 1/2 cup butter in a medium saucepan over low heat. Whisk in the broth. Cook for 10 minutes until thickened, stirring constantly. Add the wine and season with salt and white pepper; mix well. Cover and let cool. Fold in the sour cream.

Butter a baking dish. Arrange the chicken in the dish. Top with the grapes and then cover with the sauce. Bake at 325 degrees until warm. Remove from the oven.

Makes 8 servings

Anne Puckett

CORNISH HENS WITH
CORN BREAD STUFFING

*When stuffing any poultry, it's important to keep the stuffing mixture
refrigerated unless it will be used immediately.*

CORN BREAD STUFFING
1 cup diced white onion
1 cup diced unpeeled apple
1/2 cup diced celery
2 tablespoons butter
4 cups crumbled corn bread
1/2 cup pecan pieces
1 1/2 cups chicken stock
2 eggs, beaten
1 teaspoon chopped parsley
1/2 teaspoon white pepper

CORNISH HENS
4 Cornish hens
2 teaspoons garlic pepper
1 teaspoon poultry seasoning
1/2 teaspoon kosher salt
1/4 cup (1/2 stick) butter, softened
1 cup chicken stock
1/4 cup dry white wine

For the stuffing, sauté the onion, apple and celery in the butter in a large skillet for 5 to 6 minutes until the onion is translucent. Remove from the heat. Add the corn bread, pecans, stock, eggs, parsley and white pepper and mix well. Refrigerate until ready to use.

For the Cornish hens, discard the giblet pack. Rinse the hens with cold water inside and out; pat dry. Combine the garlic pepper, poultry seasoning and salt in a small bowl. Rub 1 tablespoon of the butter over each hen. Season with the garlic pepper mixture. Stuff with the stuffing. Cross the legs and tie with butcher's string. Arrange in a heavy ovenproof skillet or roasting pan. Roast at 400 degrees for 1 hour or until the juices run clear and the thickest point of the thigh registers 165 degrees on a meat thermometer.

Remove the hens from the pan. Cover with foil to keep warm. Set the skillet over medium heat and deglaze. Add the stock and wine. Cook until reduced by half. Spoon over the hens to serve.

Makes 4 servings

*Tip: Deglazing is a cooking technique for removing and
dissolving caramelized food residue from a pan to make a sauce.
To deglaze, remove any excess fat, place the pan over medium-high
heat, and scrape the caramelized bits from the bottom. Add liquid
such as stock or wine and cook until reduced by half.*

DUCK BREAST CASSOULET

4 duck breasts
1 teaspoon lemon pepper
Salt to taste
2 tablespoons soy sauce
1 tablespoon balsamic vinegar
1 teaspoon honey
1/2 cup thinly sliced onion
1 garlic clove, thinly sliced
1/2 teaspoon thyme leaves, chopped
1 (15-ounce) can cannellini beans, drained
1/4 cup chutney
(preferably Stonewall Kitchen Farmhouse Chutney)

Season the duck all over with the lemon pepper and salt. Heat an ovenproof skillet over medium-low heat. Arrange the breasts skin side down in the skillet. Cook without turning until the skin is crisp and the fat melts; drain.

Combine the soy sauce, vinegar and honey in a medium bowl. Add the duck and stir to coat. Return the duck to the skillet, skin side down. Cook until more of the fat melts; drain. Return the duck to the soy sauce mixture. Let stand.

Sauté the onion, garlic and thyme until the onion is translucent. Add the beans and duck, skin side up. Top each duck breast with 1 tablespoon of the chutney. Bake, covered, at 350 degrees for 40 minutes or until the duck registers 165 degrees on a meat thermometer. Serve with crusty bread and wilted spinach.

Makes 4 servings

In the kitchen, one of the first lessons students learn when sautéing or braising food is, "Brown it, Don't Burn it."
Chopped garlic burns quickly, so add it as the second ingredient so that it's less likely to burn. The taste of burned garlic can ruin any recipe, but a gentle browning releases a nutty, aromatic flavor. Many garlic cloves have been sacrificed on their way to a perfect dish because the pan was too hot! —The Chef

DUCK AND WILD RICE

2 packages seasoned wild and
long-grain rice blend
2 ducks
3 ribs celery
1 onion, cut into halves
1 teaspoon salt
1/2 teaspoon pepper

1/2 cup chopped onion
1 cup mushrooms, sliced
1/2 cup (1 stick) butter
1/4 cup all-purpose flour
1 1/2 cups half-and-half
1 tablespoon chopped parsley
1/4 cup slivered almonds

Prepare the rice blend according to the package directions.

Combine the ducks, celery, onion halves, salt and pepper in a large stockpot. Add water to cover. Bring to a boil; reduce the heat and cook for 20 minutes or until tender. Reserve the broth. Let the ducks cool.

Cut the breast meat from the bone. Remove the skin. Cut the duck legs from the carcass. Remove the skin from the thighs and legs. Cut the meat from the bones. Cut all the meat into cubes. There should be about 3 1/2 cups.

Sauté the chopped onion and mushrooms in the butter in a large skillet or casserole. Add the flour and mix well. Add the duck and 1 1/2 cups of the reserved broth. Cook until slightly thickened, stirring frequently. Add the rice, half-and-half and parsley and mix well.

Pour the duck mixture into a greased 2-quart baking dish. Sprinkle with the almonds. Bake, covered, at 350 degrees for 20 minutes. Uncover and bake for 10 minutes longer.

Makes 6 servings

MARYLAND CRAB CAKES

1 egg
1/4 cup mayonnaise
1 teaspoon yellow mustard
1 teaspoon Dijon mustard
1 teaspoon Worcestershire sauce
1 tablespoon lemon juice
1 teaspoon Old Bay seasoning
1 teaspoon chopped parsley
1/4 cup coarse saltine cracker crumbs
1 pound jumbo lump crab meat
Chile-Lime Tartar Sauce (page 15)

Combine the egg, mayonnaise, yellow mustard, Dijon mustard, Worcestershire sauce, lemon juice, Old Bay seasoning, parsley and cracker crumbs in a bowl and mix well. Fold in the crab meat, taking care not to break up the lumps.

Form into six equal crab cakes, pressing firmly to compact the ingredients. Bake on a lightly greased baking pan at 350 degrees for 15 minutes or until light brown. Serve with Chili Lime Tartar Sauce.

Makes 6 servings

Tip: *When cooking with jumbo lump crab meat, it is important to handle, mix, or stir it as little as possible in order to keep the crab meat lumps as large as possible.*

Oysters Johnny Reb

1/2 cup minced parsley
3/4 cup chopped green onions
Salt and pepper to taste
Tabasco sauce to taste
1 tablespoon Worcestershire sauce
2 tablespoons lemon juice
31/2 cups saltine cracker crumbs
1/2 cup (1 stick) butter, melted
2 pints oysters, drained and patted dry
1 cup half-and-half
1 teaspoon paprika
1 tablespoon butter, chilled and cut into pieces

Combine the parsley, green onions, salt, pepper, Tabasco sauce, Worcestershire sauce, lemon juice, cracker crumbs and 1/2 cup butter in a medium bowl; mix just until combined. Arrange a layer of oysters over the bottom of a greased shallow glass baking dish. Cover with one-third of the crumb mixture. Repeat with the remaining oysters and half the remaining crumb mixture. Pour the half-and-half over the top. Top with the remaining crumb mixture. Sprinkle with the paprika. Dot with 1 tablespoon cold butter. Bake at 375 degrees for 30 to 45 minutes or until brown on top and set.

Makes 8 to 10 servings

Beth Lebow

Jumbo Prawns on Rosemary Skewers

For a dramatic presentation, use long, heavy stems of rosemary to replace traditional skewers. Strip the leaves from the stems, leaving a tuft of rosemary at the end.

1/4 cup olive oil
Zest and juice of 1 lemon
1 tablespoon chopped rosemary
Salt and pepper to taste
24 jumbo prawns, peeled
4 sprigs of rosemary

Prepare a medium fire in a grill. Combine the olive oil, lemon zest, lemon juice, chopped rosemary, salt and pepper in a bowl. Add the prawns and toss to coat. Thread six prawns on each of four skewers. Grill for 3 minutes on each side. Garnish each with a rosemary sprig.

Makes 4 servings

Anne West

Tip: A great way to peel prawns and shrimp is with a small "slide through" envelope opener. It's also helpful for deveining prawns or shimp.

ADLAI STEVENSON'S SHRIMP

*Adlai Stevenson II, the thirty-first governor of Illinois,
served this dish to United Nations Secretary-General U Thant
and President John F. Kennedy when he represented the
United States as UN ambassador.*

2 (14-ounce) cans artichoke hearts, cut into eighths
4 ounces mushrooms, sliced
5 1/2 tablespoons butter
1 pound shrimp
1/4 cup all-purpose flour
1 3/4 cups milk
1/4 cup dry sherry
Salt and pepper to taste
1 tablespoon Worcestershire sauce
1/2 cup grated Parmesan cheese
1 tablespoon paprika
Hot cooked rice

Arrange the artichokes over the bottom of an 8×8-inch baking dish. Sauté the mushrooms and shrimp in 1 1/2 tablespoons of the butter in a skillet over low heat just until the shrimp begin to turn pink. Arrange over the artichokes using a slotted spoon.

Add the remaining 1/4 cup butter to the drippings in the skillet. Add the flour, whisking until combined. Whisk in the milk, sherry, salt, pepper and Worcestershire sauce until smooth and combined. Cook over low heat until thickened. Pour over the shrimp.

Sprinkle with the cheese and paprika. Bake at 350 degrees for 30 minutes or until brown and bubbly. Serve over hot cooked rice.

Makes 4 to 6 servings

Hans Mayer

LOW-COUNTRY SHRIMP BOIL

3 or 4 onions, cut into quarters
1/2 cup (1 stick) butter
1 tablespoon pepper
1 tablespoon crab boil seasoning
3 tablespoons Old Bay seasoning
24 new potatoes
12 ears of corn, cut into halves
5 pounds large shrimp
3 to 4 pounds smoked beef sausage

Bring a large stockpot of water to a boil. Add the onions, butter, pepper, crab boil seasoning and Old Bay seasoning. Boil until the mixture is very fragrant and the onions are translucent. Add the potatoes. Boil for 10 minutes. Add the corn and boil for 4 minutes. Add the shrimp and sausage. Boil for 3 to 4 minutes until the shrimp turn pink; drain. Arrange the sausage, shrimp and vegetables on a large serving platter.

Makes 8 to 10 servings

Beth Lebow

*This traditional Low-Country Shrimp Boil is perfect
for a summer feast and great for a crowd. Just unroll brown paper to
cover your table, spread the shrimp boil on the paper, and enjoy!*

Shrimp Salad with Citrus Dressing

Salt to taste
1 1/2 pounds small shrimp, peeled and tails removed
Zest and sections of 1 orange
Zest and juice of 1 lemon
1/2 cup mayonnaise
1/2 cup mayonnaise-type salad dressing
1/2 cup diced red bell pepper
1 avocado, sliced
2 teaspoons salt
1 teaspoon Old Bay seasoning
1/8 teaspoon cayenne pepper
1 tablespoon white wine vinegar
5 cups mixed field greens

Bring a medium saucepan half-filled with salted water to a boil. Add the shrimp. Cook for 4 minutes; drain. Let stand to cool.

Roughly chop the orange sections. Combine with the orange zest, lemon zest and lemon juice in a medium bowl. Add the mayonnaise and salad dressing and mix well. Fold in the bell pepper and avocado. Add the shrimp, salt, Old Bay seasoning, cayenne pepper and vinegar and mix well. Chill in the refrigerator. Serve the shrimp salad over the field greens.

Makes 6 servings

ROCKFISH WITH CRAB CHIVE BUTTER OVER SUCCOTASH

CRAB CHIVE BUTTER
1/2 cup (1 stick) butter
1 tablespoon lemon juice
1 teaspoon anchovy paste
1 teaspoon capers
1/4 teaspoon salt
1/4 teaspoon pepper
4 ounces jumbo lump crab meat
2 tablespoons chopped chives

SUCCOTASH
1/2 cup chopped onion
1 tablespoon butter
1 cup fresh corn kernels
1 cup cooked fresh lima beans
Salt and pepper to taste
1/8 teaspoon smoked paprika

ROCKFISH AND ASSEMBLY
1 1/2 pounds rockfish
Salt and pepper to taste
1 teaspoon olive oil
Chopped chives

For the butter, combine the butter, lemon juice, anchovy paste, capers, salt and pepper in a food processor. Process until creamy and well mixed. Remove to a bowl. Fold in the crab meat and chives.

For the succotash, sauté the onion in the butter in a skillet until translucent. Add the corn. Cook on medium-high heat for 1 minute. Add the lima beans. Cook for 1 minute longer. Season with salt, pepper and paprika.

For the rockfish, cut the fish into 4 equal portions. Season with salt and pepper. Sauté the fish in the olive oil in a skillet for 2 minutes per side.

Spoon the succotash onto warmed plates. Arrange the fish over the succotash. Top with a generous dollop of Crab Chive Butter. Garnish with chives.

Makes 4 servings

Katie O'Malley, Maryland's First Lady

CEDAR-PLANKED SALMON

1 (12-ounce) can beer
1/2 cup maple syrup
2 tablespoons Dijon mustard
1 tablespoon Old Bay seasoning
1 garlic clove, minced
6 (4- to 5-ounce) salmon fillets
Tomato Mango Chutney (page 173)

Combine the beer, syrup, Dijon mustard, Old Bay seasoning and garlic in a shallow dish large enough to hold the salmon fillets and marinade. Add the salmon; turn to coat. Marinate for about 1 hour.

Soak two 11-inch clean, untreated cedar planks in water for at least 1 hour. Heat a gas grill or burn charcoal until coals have an even coat of white ash.

Ensure that each fillet is well coated with marinade. Place 3 fillets on each plank. Put the planks on the grill. When the planks begin to flame around the edges, close the lid to slow the planks' burning and allow the fish to hot-smoke.

Cook the salmon for 8 to 10 minutes. Use long, sturdy tongs to remove the planks from the grill. Serve the fish on the planks for a dramatic presentation. Serve with Tomato Mango Chutney.

Makes 6 servings

Tip: You can purchase a high-quality cedar plank from any good kitchen supply store. Or, go to your local lumber department and cut 6×11-inch planks from their untreated cedar stock.

TILAPIA WITH MANGO AND LEMON BUTTER

1 mango
4 tilapia fillets
1 to 1 1/2 cups water
Salt and pepper to taste
6 tablespoons butter
Juice of 1 lemon

Cut the mango into thin strips. Arrange the fillets on a rimmed sheet pan lined with aluminum foil. Pour the water into the pan to prevent the fillets from drying out while broiling. Season with salt and pepper. Broil under low heat for 5 minutes.

Combine the mango, butter and lemon juice in a bowl. Microwave, covered, until the butter is melted. Spoon over the fish.

Makes 4 servings

MUSTARD-GLAZED FISH

2 tablespoons mayonnaise
2 teaspoons Dijon mustard
1 teaspoon lemon juice
2 fish fillets, any variety

Combine the mayonnaise, Dijon mustard and lemon juice in a small bowl and mix well. Arrange the fillets on a broiler pan. Spread the sauce over the fillets. Broil under low heat until flaky and golden brown.

Makes 2 servings

Anne West

150

TRI-COLOR PASTA SALAD

YOGURT VINAIGRETTE
1/4 cup balsamic vinegar
3/4 cup olive oil
1 tablespoon Greek yogurt
1 tablespoon chopped parsley
Salt and pepper to taste

SALAD
8 ounces asparagus, cut on the
diagonal into bite-size pieces

1 cup baby green beans, cut on the
diagonal into bite-size pieces
10 ounces fresh spinach, rinsed
2 cups tri-color pasta, cooked
al dente and drained
1 cup kalamata olives, pitted
1 cup crumbled feta cheese
1 cup grape tomatoes, cut into halves
Salt and pepper to taste

For the vinaigrette, combine the vinegar, olive oil, yogurt, parsley, salt and pepper in a bowl or a jar with a tight-fitting lid. Whisk or shake to blend.

For the salad, blanch the asparagus and green beans in boiling salted water just until they turn bright green. Drain, then place in ice water to stop the cooking process. Drain well again. Place the spinach in a large heated skillet. Cook for 1 to 2 minutes or until wilted, stirring constantly. Combine the asparagus, beans and spinach with the pasta in a large bowl and mix well. Stir in the olives, cheese, tomatoes, salt and pepper. Add the dressing and toss to coat.

Makes 6 servings

SHRIMP COCKTAIL PASTA SALAD

1 to 2 pounds shrimp, peeled
and deveined
12 ounces rotini pasta
3 ribs celery, chopped
1 onion, chopped

1 red bell pepper, chopped
2 garlic cloves, chopped
1 cup chili sauce
3 tablespoons mayonnaise
2 teaspoons horseradish

Boil the shrimp in water to cover in a stockpot until they turn pink; drain. Cook the pasta according to the package directions; drain. Rinse with cold water; drain thoroughly.

Combine the shrimp, pasta, celery, onion, bell pepper, garlic, chili sauce, mayonnaise and horseradish in a large bowl and mix well. Chill for at least 20 minutes before serving.

Makes 8 to 10 servings

Julie Ann Coyne

Lasagna with Sausage

Sausage Sauce
1 pound Italian sausage, casings removed
1 cup chopped onion
1 pound mushrooms, sliced (optional)
3 large garlic cloves, minced
2 teaspoons dried oregano
1/4 teaspoon red pepper flakes
2 tablespoons olive oil
1 (28-ounce) can crushed tomatoes
1 (15-ounce) can diced tomatoes
Salt and pepper to taste

Filling
1 1/2 cups packed fresh basil leaves
8 ounces ricotta cheese
1 1/2 cups (6 ounces) shredded
part-skim mozzarella cheese
3/4 cup (3 ounces) grated
Parmesan cheese
1 egg
1/2 teaspoon salt
1/4 teaspoon pepper

For the sauce, sauté the sausage, onion, mushrooms, garlic, oregano and pepper flakes in the olive oil in a large stockpot over medium-high heat until the sausage is browned and crumbly. Add the crushed tomatoes and undrained diced tomatoes. Bring to a boil. Reduce the heat to a simmer. Cook to blend the flavors. Season with salt and pepper.

For the filling, chop the basil by pulsing it in a food processor. Add the ricotta cheese, mozzarella cheese, Parmesan cheese, egg, salt and pepper. Process to combine.

NOODLES AND ASSEMBLY
1 (9-ounce) box no-boil lasagna noodles
3 cups (12 ounces) shredded mozzarella cheese
1 cup (4 ounces) grated
Parmesan cheese

For the assembly, spread $1/2$ cup of the sauce over the bottom of a 9×13-inch baking dish. Arrange a layer of noodles over the sauce; do not allow the noodles to touch. Spread $11/2$ cups of the filling evenly over the noodles. Sprinkle with about 1 cup of the mozzarella cheese and $1/3$ cup of the Parmesan cheese. Top with another layer of noodles, filling, sauce, $1/3$ cup Parmesan cheese and 1 cup mozzarella cheese. Top with the remaining noodles. Cover with sauce. Cover the baking dish with greased foil. Bake at 375 degrees for 40 minutes. Uncover and top with the remaining mozzarella cheese and Parmesan cheese. Bake until the cheese is light brown. Let stand 15 minutes before slicing.

Makes 8 servings

Cassie Motz

This recipe can be made vegetarian by substituting sautéed spinach for the sausage. Be sure to drain the excess liquid from the spinach. When layering the lasagna, be sure to reserve enough of the sauce and cheese to finish the top of the lasagna.

Tip: To store lasagna, spray a sheet of aluminum foil with nonstick cooking spray before covering it, which will prevent the cheese from sticking to the foil.

LASAGNA WITH SPINACH AND MUSHROOMS

SAUCE
1 onion, chopped
2 garlic cloves, chopped
5 tablespoons olive oil
1 (28-ounce) can crushed tomatoes
2 teaspoons chopped fresh basil
or parsley
Salt and pepper to taste

FILLING
1 onion, chopped
1 tablespoon olive oil

1 pound cremini, trimmed
and sliced
Salt and pepper to taste
1 tablespoon olive oil
10 ounces fresh spinach, chopped

NOODLES AND ASSEMBLY
15 no-boil lasagna noodles
4 cups (1 pound) packed shredded
part-skim mozzarella cheese
1/2 cup (2 ounces) grated
Parmesan cheese

For the sauce, sauté the onion and garlic in the olive oil in a large skillet over medium heat until the onion is translucent. Add the tomatoes. Bring to a boil. Reduce the heat and simmer for 10 minutes or until slightly thickened. Add the basil, salt and pepper. Pour the sauce into a large measuring cup. Add enough water to measure 3 1/2 cups.

For the filling, sauté the onion in 1 tablespoon olive oil in a skillet over medium until the onion is translucent. Add the mushrooms and sauté for 8 minutes or until golden brown. Season with salt and pepper. Remove the mushroom mixture to a large bowl. Add 1 tablespoon olive oil to the skillet. Add the spinach and sauté for 5 minutes or until wilted, stirring frequently. Season with salt and pepper. Combine with the mushroom mixture.

For the assembly, spread 1/2 cup of the sauce over the bottom of a greased 9×13-inch baking dish. Arrange three noodles over the sauce, not allowing the noodles to touch. Spread 3/4 cup of the filling evenly over the noodles. Spread 1/2 cup of the sauce over the filling. Sprinkle 3/4 cup of the mozzarella cheese and 2 generous tablespoons of the Parmesan cheese over the sauce. Repeat the layers three more times, taking care to reserve enough sauce and cheese for topping the final layer. Cover the lasagna with greased aluminum foil. Bake at 375 degrees for 25 to 30 minutes. Remove the foil. Bake until the cheese is brown and the sauce is bubbly. Let stand 5 minutes before slicing.

Makes 8 servings

Cassie Motz

LINGUINE AND CLAM SAUCE

3 garlic cloves, minced
1/2 cup minced shallots
3 tablespoons butter
1/4 cup olive oil
1 (2-ounce) can flat anchovies, drained
1 1/2 cups bottled clam juice
1/2 cup dry white wine
1/2 teaspoon rosemary leaves, chopped
1/2 cup flat-leaf parsley, minced
1 teaspoon pepper
2 (8-ounce) cans clams, minced
16 ounces linguine, cooked al dente and drained

Sauté the garlic and shallots in the butter and olive oil in a sauté pan until light brown. Add the anchovies. Cook until the anchovies dissolve, stirring constantly. Add the clam juice, wine, rosemary, parsley and pepper. Bring to a boil. Reduce the heat and simmer for 15 minutes. Add the clams and cook 5 minutes longer. Serve over the hot cooked linguine. For a special treat, sauté cleaned deveined shrimp in a small amount of butter, olive oil and garlic. Chop the shrimp and stir into the sauce just before serving.

Makes 6 to 8 servings

John Sabatelli

Variation: *The sauce can also be made with fresh cherrystone clams. Wash the clams thoroughly. Bring about 3 cups of water to a boil in a saucepan; add the clams, cover, and steam until the clams open. Discard any unopened clams. Remove the clams from their shells and roughly chop, reserving the juice. Increase or decrease the amount of any ingredient to taste and this sauce will still be fine. The anchovies dissolve in the sauce and are essential, not overpowering.*

SPICY SHRIMP AND LINGUINE

1 pound medium shrimp, peeled
and deveined
Old Bay seasoning to taste
1/4 cup extra-virgin olive oil
1 Vidalia onion, diced
4 or 5 garlic cloves, minced
8 ounces button mushrooms,
sliced (optional)
1 green bell pepper, chopped
2 (15-ounce) cans
petite-diced tomatoes
1/2 to 3/4 cup dry white wine

1 tablespoon Italian seasoning
Salt and pepper to taste
1 teaspoon red pepper flakes
(optional)
1/4 cup chiffonade of basil
16 ounces linguine, cooked
al dente and drained
Freshly grated Parmesan cheese
to taste
2 tablespoons chopped
flat-leaf parsley

Season the shrimp with Old Bay seasoning. Sauté in 2 tablespoons of the olive oil in a sauté pan for 1 to 2 minutes per side until pink. Remove from the pan using a slotted spoon.

Heat the remaining 2 tablespoons olive oil in the pan. Add the onion and sauté until translucent. Add the garlic, mushrooms and bell pepper. Sauté until tender. Add the undrained tomatoes, wine, Italian seasoning, salt and pepper. Bring to a boil. Reduce the heat and simmer for 25 to 30 minutes. Add red pepper flakes, basil and shrimp. Simmer until the shrimp are heated through, but do not overcook. Serve over the linguine. Top with Parmesan and parsley.

Makes 4 servings

Belinda Waterman

Variation: *This dish can also be made with chicken, or with a combination of chicken and shrimp.*

SHRIMP MAC' AND CHEESE

1 tablespoon olive oil
2 cups macaroni, cooked al dente and drained
8 ounces Velveeta cheese
8 ounces cream cheese
1 1/2 cups chicken stock
3/4 cup half-and-half
1/8 teaspoon cayenne pepper
1 teaspoon white pepper
Salt to taste
1 1/2 cups (6 ounces) shredded sharp white Cheddar cheese
1 1/2 pounds (21- to 25-count) shrimp, peeled and deveined

Stir the olive oil into the drained macaroni. Set the pasta aside, but stir occasionally.

Combine the Velveeta, cream cheese and stock in a heavy-bottomed saucepan. Cook over moderate heat until the cheeses begin to melt, stirring frequently. Add the half-and-half, cayenne pepper, white pepper and salt. Cook over low heat, stirring frequently to prevent scorching.

Combine the pasta with the Cheddar cheese in a large bowl. Add the cheese sauce and mix well. Pour into a greased 9×9-inch baking dish. Bake at 350 degrees for 25 to 30 minutes until the cheese is bubbly.

Steam the shrimp. Remove the tails, if desired. Stir the shrimp into the mac' and cheese before serving.

Makes 6 to 8 servings

Tip: For another trendy version of mac' and cheese,
add lobster. Or you can go with the "kid-loved" traditional
and not add anything.

ORZO AND GRILLED CHICKEN

GRILLED CHICKEN AND VEGETABLES
3 tablespoons olive oil
1/4 cup balsamic vinegar
1 teaspoon dried oregano
1/2 teaspoon kosher salt
1/2 teaspoon pepper
1 pound boneless chicken thighs
2 zucchini, cut diagonally into 1-inch pieces
1 large red onion, cut into quarters and separated

ORZO
1 cup orzo
1 pint grape tomatoes, cut into halves
3 tablespoons chopped basil
1/2 cup (2 ounces) grated Parmesan cheese
1/4 cup olive oil
Kosher salt and pepper to taste

For the chicken, set a large sealable plastic bag in a bowl. Combine the olive oil, vinegar, oregano, salt and pepper in the bag. Add the chicken, zucchini and onion. Marinate in the refrigerator for at least 30 minutes.

Grill the chicken over medium heat for about 8 minutes per side or until an internal temperature of 165 degrees is reached, turning occasionally.

Arrange the zucchini and onion on a grill pan. Grill to ensure grill marks on both sides of the vegetables, turning once.

For the orzo, cook the orzo to al dente according to the package directions. Remove to a large serving bowl. Add the grilled zucchini and onion and all their juices; the tomatoes, basil and cheese. Drizzle with the olive oil. Toss to combine. Season with salt and pepper. Serve with the chicken.

Makes 4 servings

A.J. Furay

BAKED ZITI

6 cups Marinara Sauce (page 185)
2 teaspoons dried Italian seasoning
4 cups ziti, cooked al dente and drained
3 cups (12 ounces) shredded part-skim mozzarella cheese
1 large egg
16 ounces ricotta cheese
1/4 cup (1 ounce) grated Parmesan cheese
1 teaspoon dried parsley flakes
1/2 teaspoon salt

Combine the Marinara Sauce and Italian seasoning and mix well. Reserve 2 cups of the sauce. Combine the remaining sauce with the pasta in a bowl.

Pour half the pasta mixture into a lightly greased 3-quart baking dish. Sprinkle with 1 cup of the mozzarella.

Beat the egg in a medium bowl. Add the ricotta cheese, Parmesan cheese, parsley and salt and mix well. Spread over the cheese layer. Top with the remaining pasta mixture. Sprinkle with 1 cup of the remaining mozzarella cheese. Spread the reserved 2 cups marinara sauce over the top, spreading to the edges.

Bake at 350 degrees for 30 minutes until heated through. Sprinkle with the remaining 1 cup mozzarella cheese. Return to the oven for 3 to 5 minutes until the cheese is melted and just a bit brown in spots.

Makes 4 to 6 servings

Bruce Kirby

Professional kitchens can be intimidating. I expose students to real work experiences by teaming them with my professional catering staff. Over the last five years, students have had opportunities to work events that have served from 150 to 1,000 guests. Working under pressure, exact timing, and preparing large quantities of food helps students learn how to keep their cool. —The Chef

GNOCCHI WITH TRIO OF CHEESES

GNOCCHI
2 pounds russet potatoes
1/4 cup all-purpose flour
2 egg yolks
1/2 teaspoon lemon zest
1/2 teaspoon salt
Salt to taste
1/4 cup olive oil

CHEESE SAUCE AND ASSEMBLY
3 cups chicken stock
8 ounces cream cheese
1 teaspoon white pepper
Pinch of nutmeg
1/2 cup (2 ounces) shredded
    mozzarella cheese
1/2 cup (2 ounces) shredded
    Parmesan cheese
1/2 cup (2 ounces) shredded
    romano cheese
1/4 cup chiffonade of basil

Bake the potatoes. Cut into halves and let cool completely. Peel the potatoes and press through a ricer. Combine the riced potatoes with the flour, egg yolks, lemon zest and 1/2 teaspoon salt. Work the dough just until blended. (Overworking the dough can result in tough gnocchi).

Turn the dough onto a floured board. Divide the dough into three portions. Roll each portion into a rope 1 inch in diameter. Cut off 1-inch pieces of dough. Press each piece with the tines of a fork to make a slight indentation.

Fill a 4-quart saucepan half-full with salted water. Add the olive oil. Bring to a boil. Add about fifteen of the gnocchi. Cook for several minutes until they float. Remove with a slotted spoon. Repeat with the remaining gnocchi.

For the cheese sauce, bring the stock to a boil in a heavy saucepan. Stir in the cream cheese, white pepper and nutmeg with a wire whisk until blended. Reduce the heat. Add the gnocchi and cook until heated through. Add the mozzarella, Parmesan and romano cheeses and mix gently. Garnish with the basil. Serve immediately.

Makes 4 to 6 servings

Tip: A chiffonade is a fine cut of leafy greens used for garnish. Remove the stems from several basil leaves and stack them together on a cutting board. With a sharp knife, cut the stacked leaves into very thin strips.

BARLEY, CORN, AND TOMATO SALAD

2¹/2 cups water
1 teaspoon salt
1 cup barley
¹/4 cup champagne vinegar

³/4 cup fresh basil, rinsed and dried
¹/3 cup canola oil
2 cups roasted corn (4 ears)
1 pint cherry tomatoes, cut into halves

Bring the water and salt to a boil in a saucepan. Stir in the barley. Cover and simmer for 20 minutes until tender. Remove to a large bowl; let cool. Combine the vinegar, basil and canola oil in a blender or food processor. Process until emulsified. Add the corn, tomatoes and dressing to the barley. Chill in the refrigerator.

Makes 8 to 10 servings

Alan Morestein, Regi's American Bistro

Tip: Roast corn by cutting the kernels from the cobs. Sear in a dry sauté pan until some of the kernels begin to brown. Reduce the heat. Add ¹/4 cup water. Cover and cook for 5 minutes.

CREAMY CHEESE POLENTA

1 shallot, minced
1 tablespoon butter
2¹/2 cups (or more) chicken stock
1 cup polenta
4 ounces cream cheese

2 tablespoons chopped parsley
¹/2 teaspoon white pepper
1 cup (4 ounces) shredded sharp
   white Cheddar cheese

Sauté the shallot in the butter in a saucepan. Add the stock and bring to a boil. Add the polenta, cream cheese, parsley and white pepper. Reduce the heat and cook for 3 to 5 minutes until the polenta thickens. Add additional stock if needed to reach the consistency of cream of wheat. Add the Cheddar cheese just before serving.

Makes 6 servings

QUINOA SALAD

Quinoa is often thought to be a whole grain. However, it is actually a seed that can be prepared like other grains such as rice and barley. Generally found in the Andes Mountains of South America, it is known as the "Mother Grain," as its ancient roots reflect the respect with which the Inca held it.

ORANGE MUSTARD VINAIGRETTE
1/2 cup olive oil
1/4 cup balsamic vinegar
1/2 cup orange juice
1/8 teaspoon cayenne pepper
1/4 cup honey mustard dressing

QUINOA
2 shallots, minced
1/2 teaspoon minced garlic
1 tablespoon olive oil
1 cup white or red quinoa, rinsed

2 1/4 cups chicken stock
1/2 teaspoon salt
1/2 teaspoon white pepper

VEGETABLES
1 cup peeled sweet potatoes, diced into confetti-size pieces
Salt to taste
1 cup haricots verts (baby green beans), diced into confetti-size pieces
Zest and sections of 3 oranges
1/2 cup dried cherries, diced

For the dressing, combine olive oil, vinegar, orange juice, cayenne pepper and dressing in a bowl or a jar with a tight-fitting lid. Whisk or shake to combine.

For the quinoa, sauté the shallots and garlic in the olive oil in a saucepan until translucent. Add the quinoa and stock. Bring to a simmer. Reduce the heat to low. Cook, covered, for 30 minutes.

For the vegetables, boil the sweet potatoes in salted water until tender. Add the haricots verts and cook for 2 minutes; drain. Plunge the vegetables into a bowl of ice water to stop the cooking process. Drain and pat dry.

Combine the quinoa, vegetables, orange zest, orange sections and cherries in a bowl. Add the dressing and toss to combine.

Makes 6 servings

Tip: The exterior of quinoa seed is covered with saponin, which can be bitter. Read the package to be sure that the quinoa is prewashed. If you're using red quinoa, it may need to cook a few minutes longer.

BRAZILIAN RICE AND BEANS

1¹/2 cups dried pinto beans
8 cups water
2 pounds smoked beef sausage, sliced
8 cups water
3 garlic cloves, minced
2 to 3 teaspoons olive oil or vegetable oil
1 chicken bouillon cube, crushed
Hot cooked rice

Soak the beans in 8 cups water for at least 8 hours; drain. Combine the beans, sausage and 8 cups water in a pressure cooker. Lock the lid. Bring to a boil. Cook for 35 minutes from the time the cooker begins to steam. Release the pressure quickly. Open the pot carefully. Simmer, uncovered, over low heat. Mash the beans in the cooking water to thicken the liquid.

Sauté the garlic in the olive oil in a skillet. Stir in the bouillon cube. Add a ladleful of the bean mixture to the skillet. Simmer for 1 minute.

Pour the contents of the skillet into the beans. Stir to combine. Simmer until the liquid thickens. If it becomes too thick, add a small amount of hot water. Serve over hot cooked rice.

Makes 8 servings

Rodrigo Neder

Beans and rice is a staple in Brazil. One of the most flavorful and popular bouillons is Knorr brand, which can also be found in the United States. Traditionally this is served with roasted meats such as pork or chicken.

CHINESE FRIED RICE

2 cups rice, cooked and chilled
2 green onions, finely chopped
2 to 3 tablespoons vegetable oil
2 eggs, beaten

1 tablespoon soy sauce, or to taste
1/2 teaspoon cayenne pepper
2 bacon slices, crisp-cooked and
finely chopped

Fry the rice and green onions in the oil in a hot skillet or wok until the rice is heated through. Add the eggs and cook until eggs are set, stirring constantly. Add the soy sauce, cayenne pepper and bacon. Adjust the seasonings to taste before serving.

Make 4 servings

Mary Lou Mullen

Tip: Most grains and rice are prepared using two parts liquid to one part grain. Vary this recipe by using cooked chicken, beef, pork, lobster, shrimp, ham, or crab meat.

SAFFRON RICE

1 shallot, minced
1 tablespoon butter
1 1/2 cups long-grain white rice

Pinch of saffron threads
3 cups chicken stock
1/2 teaspoon salt

Sauté the shallot in the butter in a saucepan. Add the rice and saffron and stir to coat. Add the stock and salt and bring to a boil. Reduce the heat to low. Steam, covered, for 14 minutes. Let stand for 5 minutes before uncovering.

Makes 6 servings

Risotto with a Trio of Mushrooms

2 tablespoons chopped shallots
1 cup arborio rice
$1/2$ teaspoon kosher salt
1 tablespoon olive oil
5 cups chicken stock
8 ounces mixed oyster, shiitake and baby bella mushrooms
2 tablespoons butter
$1/2$ cup white wine
$1/2$ cup (2 ounces) grated
Parmesan cheese

Sauté the shallots, rice and salt in the olive oil in a saucepan for 4 to 5 minutes until the shallots begin to become tender. Add 1 cup of the stock. Cook until the stock is mostly absorbed but the mixture appears creamy, stirring constantly. Continue adding stock 1 cup at a time and stirring as it cooks. The entire process will take about 25 minutes and result in a creamy rice.

Sauté the mushrooms in the butter in a skillet for several minutes until tender. Add the wine. Cook for several minutes longer. Add the mushrooms and their liquid to the risotto just before serving. Stir in the cheese. Serve immediately.

Makes 4 to 6 servings

Tip: Unlike cooking traditional rice, arborio is sautéed in hot oil prior to adding liquid and must be stirred constantly while cooking. This method releases the starches of the rice that make risotto so creamy. Cheese will clump and stick to the pan if added too soon, so add it at the last minute.

CONDIMENTS & SAUCES

Bill Wilson

*"Having a job and going to work everyday is like moving from
the darkness into the light. It is being a regular person again. I love my job
and look forward to going to work."*

Denise

Culinary arts graduate, employed for six years

Employment and Job Training Programs

BOS's goal is to stop the cycle of homelessness and promote lasting solutions to maintaining self-sufficiency. However, there are many barriers to securing employment. Forty percent of our clients have substance abuse problems or significant mental health issues. Nine percent are employed, with two percent earning more than minimum wage and no one receiving health care benefits. Twenty-four percent did not complete high school.

Our Employment Development Specialist meets with each woman in the shelter, conducting an assessment including education, job skills, and work history. Residents are enrolled in GED classes and computer skills training, and referrals are made to job training programs. Residents are assisted in preparing resumes and conducting job searches online.

In 2005 BOS began culinary arts training to provide a viable skill set to help move residents to employment. Culinary arts training is an eight-week program developed and taught on site by Chef Connie Crabtree-Burritt. Chef Crabtree-Burritt is an experienced restauranteur and culinary art instructor. She has a passion for taking a woman who is a natural cook or is willing to try and giving her a skill set so she can support her family. The curriculum focuses on teaching the basic skills and knowledge needed for employment in a commercial kitchen at the level of beginning prep cook. The Sanitation and Food Safety Certification Program is incorporated into the curriculum.

Since 2005 one hundred women have completed culinary arts training in intensive six- to eight-person groups. Sixty percent of the women have reported obtaining employment. In 2011, in an effort to move more women to employment, an eight-week internship in local restaurants following graduation from culinary arts training began.

DRESSED FOR DINNER

Menu

Crème Baltimore

Rosemary Grilled Chicken with Tomato Mango Chutney

Brussels Sprouts with Marmalade Glaze

Potatoes Au Gratin

*Caramel and Salted Almond Tapenade
over Brie cheese with ginger snaps*

Chocolate Raspberry Bars

*Condiments and sauces can make all the difference in your meal.
A menu full of surprises for the more adventurous eater is a true delight.
Jumbo lump crab meat goes a long way in this unique cold soup.
Ending the meal with the flavors packed in this sweet and savory tapenade
served with creamy brie make for dinner with style.*

RED PEPPER AÏOLI

6 garlic cloves
1 teaspoon salt
1/4 teaspoon cayenne pepper
1/3 cup chopped peeled roasted red
bell pepper

1/3 cup fresh white bread crumbs
1 tablespoon lemon juice
1 egg yolk
1 cup olive oil

Pound the garlic, salt and cayenne pepper to a paste in a mortar with a pestle. Add the bell pepper and pound to a smooth consistency.

Remove to a food processor. Add the bread crumbs, lemon juice and egg yolk. Pulse for several seconds. Drizzle in the oil with the motor running. Process at high speed until the mixture is the consistency of mayonnaise.

Makes 1 1/2 cups

Tip: Red Pepper Aïoli is excellent with any seafood and is a special treat as a crudite dip or spread on crusty bread.

TOMATO MANGO CHUTNEY

1 cup diced white onion
2 teaspoons minced garlic
1/2 tablespoon olive oil
3 1/2 cups canned petite-diced
tomatoes
2 cups golden raisins, chopped

1 1/2 cups mango chutney
3 tablespoons balsamic vinegar
2 tablespoons mustard seeds
1 teaspoon red pepper flakes
2 teaspoons garlic pepper

Sauté the onion and garlic in the oil until onion is translucent. Add the undrained tomatoes. Lower the heat. Simmer until the liquid is reduced by half. Add the raisins, chutney, vinegar, mustard seeds, pepper flakes and garlic pepper. Simmer until the mixture is thick and jamlike. Let cool, then chill in the refrigerator for up to 4 weeks.

Makes 3 cups

Tip: This chutney is excellent with chicken, salmon, roasted pork, and lamb.

Avocado Salad Dressing

$^1/_2$ cup olive oil
$^3/_4$ teaspoon dry mustard
$^1/_4$ teaspoon Tabasco sauce
$^1/_3$ cup lemon juice
$^1/_2$ teaspoon salt
2 avocados, diced

4 green onions, chopped
1 garlic clove, minced
4 anchovy fillets, drained,
   or to taste
$^1/_2$ cup mayonnaise

Combine the olive oil, dry mustard, Tabasco sauce, lemon juice, salt, avocados, green onions, garlic, anchovies and mayonnaise in a food processor or blender. Process until smooth and creamy. Chill for at least 2 hours. Serve as a dip, with vegetables, on salad greens or on a favorite sandwich.

Makes 2 cups

Betty Higman

Balsamic Dressing

$^1/_4$ cup balsamic vinegar
1 teaspoon Dijon mustard
2 garlic cloves, roasted and minced

$^1/_4$ teaspoon pepper
Salt to taste
$1^1/_4$ cups light olive oil

Combine the vinegar, Dijon mustard, garlic, pepper and salt in a bowl. Whisk in the olive oil gradually until well combined.

Makes $1^1/_2$ cups

Tip: *The standard ratio in oil and vinegar dressings is three parts oil to one part vinegar.*

Freezer Blackberry Jelly

*This jelly allows you to keep the freshness of the summer available
in the freezer all year long. It can be used on toast, as an
ice cream topping, or in smoothies. Once defrosted, it will keep in the
refrigerator for up to one month. You can substitute fresh
strawberries or peaches in season.*

3 quarts blackberries, freshly picked if possible
5 1/4 cups sugar (no substitutions)
1 package fruit pectin
3/4 cup water

Crush the blackberries 1 cup at a time by pressing through a sieve or using a potato masher. Discard the crushed berries. Measure exactly 3 cups of blackberry juice into a 6- to 8-quart saucepan. Add up to 1/2 cup additional water if needed to reach 3 cups of juice.

Add the sugar to the juice in the saucepan. Cook over low heat until the sugar dissolves, stirring constantly. Let the mixture stand for 10 minutes, stirring occasionally.

Combine the pectin with the water in a small saucepan. Stir until the pectin is dissolved. Bring to a boil. Boil for 1 minute, stirring constantly. Add to the blackberry mixture and mix well. Heat over low heat for 2 to 3 minutes. Pour into freezer-safe plastic containers, leaving 1/2 inch of space at the top. Let stand at room temperature for 24 hours or until jelly is firm. Store in the refrigerator for up to 3 weeks or freeze for up to 1 year.

Makes 6 half-pints

Mary Graul

***Tip:** If the jelly should crystallize in the refrigerator,
transfer it to a glass container and place uncovered
in a saucepan of hot water, stirring occasionally. This will
dissolve the sugar crystals.*

Red Onion and Bacon Marmalade

3 cups julienned red onions
1 garlic clove, minced
1 teaspoon olive oil
1/2 cup red wine
1/3 cup red wine vinegar

1/2 cup brown sugar
Zest and juice of 1 orange
1/4 cup honey
6 bacon slices, cooked and
    chopped (optional)

Sauté the onions and garlic in the olive oil in a large sauté pan until tender. Add the wine, vinegar, brown sugar, orange zest, orange juice and honey. Reduce the heat. Simmer for about 20 minutes or until the mixture reaches a jamlike consistency. Add the bacon. Let cool. Store in a airtight container for up to 2 weeks.

Makes 2 to 3 cups

Tip: Marmalade is good served with cold sliced pork on crusty bread or as an accompaniment for roasted chicken. It can also be used as a topping for a simple chèvre (goat cheese) tart.

Mango Chutney Mayonnaise

1 cup mango chutney
1 1/2 cups mayonnaise
1 tablespoon Tiger sauce

Pulse the chutney in a food processor. Add the mayonnaise and Tiger sauce and mix well.

Makes 2 1/2 cups

Chutney mayonnaise keeps well in the refrigerator for several weeks. Spread on sandwiches and wraps, especially on roasted chicken, pork, or lamb sandwiches.

SPINACH PESTO

10 to 12 ounces fresh spinach
1 cup pine nuts, toasted (see Tip below)
1/2 cup (2 ounces) grated Parmesan cheese
1 garlic clove, crushed
1/2 teaspoon white pepper
1/2 teaspoon nutmeg
1 3/4 cups (about) olive oil

Remove any large stems from the spinach. Wash thoroughly to remove any sand in the leaves. Roll in paper towels to dry.

Pulse the spinach and pine nuts in a food processor. Add the cheese, garlic, white pepper and nutmeg. Drizzle in the olive oil gradually with the motor running. Blend until smooth but not oily. It may be necessary to use more or less of the oil.

Makes 3 cups

Tip: To toast pine nuts, place them in a skillet. Toast over medium heat for several minutes until the nuts are evenly brown, stirring constantly. Pine nuts contain natural oils and therefore require no additional oil in the toasting process.

WALNUT PESTO

2 cups walnuts
5 cups fresh basil leaves,
stems removed
1 garlic clove, crushed

1 cup (4 ounces) grated
Parmesan cheese
2 cups (about) olive oil

Pulse the walnuts, basil and garlic in a blender or a food processor until roughly chopped. Add the cheese. Pour in the olive oil gradually with the motor running. Process until the mixture is smooth but not oily.

Makes 5 cups

*Tip: This pesto can be added to Cream Cheese Sauce (page 183)
or drizzled over cheese.*

PICO DE GALLO

1 large tomato, chopped
1 onion, chopped
2 jalapeño chiles, seeded and
finely chopped
1/4 cup fresh cilantro, chopped

1 garlic clove, crushed
2 teaspoons lime juice
1/2 teaspoon salt
1/2 teaspoon pepper

Combine the tomato, onion, jalapeños, cilantro, garlic, lime juice, salt and pepper in a medium bowl and mix well. Refrigerate for at least 3 hours before serving to allow the flavors to blend.

Makes 1 cup

Karen Adkins

Tip: Wear gloves when cleaning and/or chopping jalapeño chiles.

CREAM CHEESE SAUCE

24 ounces cream cheese
2 cups chicken stock
1 cup heavy cream
1/2 teaspoon salt
1/2 teaspoon white pepper
1/4 teaspoon nutmeg

Melt the cream cheese with the stock in a heavy saucepan over low heat, whisking constantly with a large wire whisk to prevent burning or sticking. Whisk in the cream, salt, white pepper and nutmeg. Simmer briefly.

Makes 6 cups

The sauce can be finished in many ways. Add pesto, Parmesan cheese, sautéed spinach, etc. It is our favorite base for pasta sauces and scalloped potatoes.

5-MINUTE HOLLANDAISE SAUCE

3 egg yolks
2 tablepoons lemon juice
1/4 teaspoon salt
Pinch of cayenne pepper
1 cup (2 sticks) butter

Combine the egg yolks, lemon juice, salt and cayenne pepper in a blender. Melt the butter over high heat until hot and bubbly. Cover the blender container and process the egg mixture for 3 seconds. Remove the center of the blender lid. Set the blender on high speed. Pour in the hot butter in a slow, steady stream. The sauce should thicken when all the butter has been added. If not, continue blending for 5 seconds longer.

Makes 1 1/2 cups

Bill Van Dyke

Tip: *Hollandaise sauce is a delicious addition to grilled or steamed asparagus and is lovely with seafood.*

GARLIC-INFUSED OIL

*This infused oil is very versatile. It can be used to sauté
meats and vegetables, tossed with cubed bread for croutons, or used
to grill your favorite panini or sandwich. It can be stored in the
refrigerator for several weeks. A few seconds in the microwave
will bring it back to an "oil" consistency.*

1 cup (2 sticks) butter
1 tablespoon minced garlic
1 1/2 cups extra-virgin olive oil
2 teaspoons Italian seasoning
1 teaspoon garlic pepper
1 tablespoon parsley, chopped

Melt the butter with the garlic over medium heat until bubbly and fragrant. Add the olive oil, Italian seasoning, garlic pepper and parsley. Remove from the heat. Store in an airtight container.

Makes 2 cups

*Tip: For the best bread crumbs ever, brush Garlic-Infused
Oil over dry bread, then toast in a 250-degree oven until crisp. Cool
completely. Pulse in a food processor to fine crumbs.*

MARINARA SAUCE

1 tablespoon minced garlic
1 tablespoon olive oil
2 (13-ounce) cans tomato purée
2 tablespoons tomato paste

1/2 teaspoon Italian seasoning
1/3 cup dry red wine
1/3 cup sugar
Salt and pepper to taste

Simmer the garlic in the olive oil in a saucepan until fragrant. Add the tomato purée and tomato paste. Simmer briefly. Add the Italian seasoning, wine, sugar, salt and pepper. Simmer over low heat for 30 to 45 minutes. For a spicier sauce, add dried red pepper flakes.

Makes 2 1/2 cups

Cathy Wood-Rupert

STRAWBERRY JALAPEÑO BARBECUE SAUCE

1 (10-ounce) package frozen
strawberries, thawed
1 1/2 cups barbecue sauce
1/2 cup ketchup
1 tablespoon molasses

1/2 tablespoon Tiger sauce
1/2 teaspoon garlic pepper
1 jalapeño chile, seeded
and chopped

Purée the strawberries in a food processor or blender until smooth. Combine the barbecue sauce, ketchup, molasses, Tiger sauce and garlic pepper in a saucepan. Bring to a simmer over low heat. Add the puréed strawberries and cook until the mixture is thick. Add the jalapeño. Chill, covered, in the refrigerator for up to 2 weeks.

Makes 2 cups

DESSERTS

David Herman

*"I support BOS because it not only provides emergency shelter,
it also allows women and children to "catch their breath" because it is a
nuturing and supportive environment. Because of BOS's commitment to counseling,
education, and job training, women are given the tools to begin moving forward.
Lives are transformed in the process!"*

Emily

Financial Contributor

THE FUTURE

During our first decade, BOS served over 2,500 women and children. Two Baltimore-area emergency shelters for women and children have closed. Today, there are fewer beds in the area than ten years ago. At the same time, the need has increased—women and children are the fastest growing segment of the homeless population nationwide. Locally, women and children make up 43 percent of the homeless population.

With the strong support of the broader community, BOS has come a long way in raising the resources necessary to "set our table." Ten years ago our church struggled to meet the first year's needs, raising $140,000 from private donations to supplement $100,000 in government funding. Today folks from a variety of groups throughout the Baltimore metropolitan area work together to raise the $980,000 needed annually to provide our much-needed services. Board and community members donate their skills and talents to help Baltimore Outreach Services meet its goals and deliver on its commitments to our residents. Many families also volunteer to help our families in need, especially during the holiday season. Corporate donors and foundations have joined in partnership with Baltimore Outreach Services to help build our programs and add to our units of supportive housing.

This cookbook connects you to our work in a very real sense. Food has traditionally provided a gathering point for sharing and fellowship in families and communities. Many community groups and people of various faith traditions prepare and serve meals at the shelter. Learning to cook in a commercial kitchen has provided job skills for over a hundred women so that they can support their families.

As you prepare a recipe from this book, we hope you think of the lives of those we are able to help with your support. With your help, Baltimore Outreach Services will continue to serve this vulnerable population of homeless women and children who have great needs and few resources, helping them move to independent lives. Thank you for joining in partnership with us.

Karen Adkins
Executive Director

SATURDAY NIGHT WITH FRIENDS

Menu

Cocktail Meatballs with Strawberry Jalapeño Sauce

Lobster Spoons

Spinach Salad

*Savory Cheesecake with Polenta Crust and
Gorgonzola Cream Cheese Sauce*

Butter Pecan Cookies

Petite Cherry Pies and Coconut Cream Pies

*Change things up, and use your baking skills in a new way.
Cheesecake as the main course is unexpected!*

*Take dessert to a new size—and use individual (miniature) pies
to allow your guests several options. Saturday night is the perfect
time to indulge with friends.*

BAKLAVA

SIMPLE SYRUP

4 cups sugar
4 cups water
2 tablespoons fresh lemon juice
1 cinnamon stick

BAKLAVA

1 pound walnuts, minced
1/2 cup almonds, minced
3/4 cup sugar
1/2 cup bread crumbs
1/2 teaspoon nutmeg
1/2 teaspoon cinnamon
24 sheets phyllo dough
1 1/2 cups (3 sticks) butter, melted

For the simple syrup, combine the sugar and water in a medium saucepan. Heat until the sugar is dissolved. Add the lemon juice and cinnamon stick. Bring to a boil. Reduce the heat and simmer for 10 minutes. Let cool completely; remove the cinnamon stick.

For the baklava, combine the walnuts, almonds, sugar, bread crumbs, nutmeg and cinnamon and mix well.

Place one sheet of the phyllo in a buttered 12×18-inch shallow baking pan. Brush with the melted butter. Repeat until there are 8 layers of phyllo. Spread half the nut mixture over the phyllo. Top with another 8 layers of buttered phyllo. Spread with the remaining nut mixture. Finish with 8 layers of buttered phyllo. Score the phyllo diagonally in both directions to form a diamond pattern. Sprinkle with a few drops of water.

Bake at 325 degrees for 1 hour until golden brown. Let stand for 5 minutes. Spoon the cooled simple syrup over the hot baklava. Let stand for at least 3 hours or until the syrup is absorbed.

Makes 8 to 10 servings

Anna Epislantis

Tip: When working with phyllo dough, it is extremely important to keep the sheets moist while preparing your dish. Place a damp dish towel over the dough until you are ready to butter an individual sheet.

CHEESECAKE SQUARES

¹/3 cup brown sugar
¹/2 cup walnuts, finely chopped
1 cup all-purpose flour
¹/3 cup butter, melted
8 ounces cream cheese, softened
¹/4 cup sugar
1 egg
1 tablespoon lemon juice
1 tablespoon milk
2 teaspoons vanilla extract

Combine the brown sugar, walnuts and flour in a medium bowl and mix well. Add the butter and mix until the mixture has a crumbly consistency. Reserve 1 cup for the topping. Press the remaining crumble mixture over the bottom of an 8×8-inch pan. Bake at 350 degrees for 12 to 15 minutes. Maintain the oven temperature.

Beat the cream cheese and sugar in a medium bowl until well bended. Add the egg, lemon juice, milk and vanilla and mix well. Spread over the baked crust. Top with the reserved 1 cup crumble mixture. Bake for 25 minutes. Cool completely. Refrigerate until cold. Cut into squares.

Makes 24 squares

Mary Graul

Tip: *For the best results, cream cheese and eggs should be brought to room temperature before mixing them with other ingredients.*

FRUIT COBBLER

1/2 cup (1 stick) butter
1 cup all-purpose flour
1/2 cup sugar
2 teaspoons baking powder

1/2 cup milk
4 cups berries or sliced fresh fruit
1/4 cup sugar

Melt the butter in a 21/2-quart baking dish. Combine the flour, 1/2 cup sugar and the baking powder in a mixing bowl. Add the milk and mix well. Pour over the butter in the baking dish; do not stir. Combine the fruit with 1/4 cup sugar in a bowl. Spoon over the batter; do not stir. Bake at 350 degrees for 45 to 55 minutes.

Makes 6 to 8 servings

Anne Puckett

Tip: For the best results, use berries or stone fruits such as peaches, plums, or nectarines for the cobbler.

DESSERT CREPES

1 cup all-purpose flour
2 cups milk

2 eggs
Vegetable oil

Combine the flour, milk and eggs in a bowl and mix well. Heat an 8-inch nonstick crepe pan. Coat lightly with oil. Pour in just enough batter to cover the bottom of the pan, tilting the pan while pouring. Cook for 1 to 2 minutes until the crepe is set and the bottom is light brown. Turn and cook for 30 to 40 seconds. Cook all the crepes in the same manner, oiling the pan between crepes.

Serve with butter and maple syrup for a classic taste, or fill with fruit, jam, chocolate chips or Nutella and sliced bananas.

Gregg Landry

CHOCOLATE FUDGE

3 tablespoons butter
2/3 cup evaporated milk
1 1/2 cups sugar
1/4 teaspoon salt
2 cups miniature marshmallows
2 cups (12 ounces) chocolate chips
1/2 cup walnuts or pecans, chopped
1 teaspoon vanilla

Combine the butter, evaporated milk, sugar and salt in a medium saucepan. Bring to a boil over medium heat, stirring constantly. Boil for 5 minutes, stirring constantly. Remove from the heat. Stir in the marshmallows, chocolate chips, walnuts and vanilla until the chocolate chips melt and the mixture is well combined. Pour into a foil-lined 8×8-inch pan. Chill until firm. Cut into 1 1/2-inch squares.

Makes 12 squares

Sylvia Weaver

When preparing our Culinary Graduation Dinner, a student once asked, "Chef, what do I say this class is about when I talk to a possible employer?" When I developed this class, I wanted to expose my students to any and every culinary experience I could. What I said to my student was, "This class is about being confident. You've learned how to blanch and sauté, the importance of being on time, and how to work as a team. An interview will be the time for you to convey that confidence and share your experiences with that possible employer." —The Chef

KEY LIME DIP AND CINNAMON CRISPS

DIP
1 (14-ounce) can sweetened condensed milk
Zest and juice of 3 limes
1 cup bottled Key lime juice
3 cups whipped topping

CINNAMON CRISPS
2 cups sugar
2 tablespoons cinnamon
8 flour tortillas
4 cups vegetable oil

For the dip, combine the sweetened condensed milk, lime zest, fresh lime juice and Key lime juice in a bowl. Chill for at least 2 hours. Fold in the whipped topping. Chill until ready to serve.

For the crisps, combine the sugar and cinnamon in a large bowl. Cut the tortillas into bite-size pieces. Fry the tortilla pieces in the hot oil in a saucepan or Dutch oven until crisp and golden brown; drain. Toss the warm chips in the cinnamon-sugar. Cool before serving with the dip.

Makes 8 to 10 servings

*Key Lime Dip is perfect for any party. Guests can
spoon this fluffy custard on their plates, or pass by and dip a few
cinnamon crisps. Serve in an oversized martini glass
for a festive presentation.*

NATILLAS (MEXICAN VANILLA CUSTARD)

CUSTARD
4 eggs yolks
1/4 cup all-purpose flour
4 cups milk
3/4 cup sugar
1/8 teaspoon salt
4 egg whites

TOPPING
1 cup heavy whipping cream
1/4 cup sugar
1/2 teaspoon vanilla extract
Nutmeg to taste

For the custard, combine the egg yolks, flour and 1 cup of the milk in a bowl to make a paste. Scald the remaining 3 cups milk with the sugar and salt in a medium saucepan over medium heat.

Add the egg yolk paste to the milk mixture. Cook over medium heat until the consistency of soft custard. Cool to room temperature. Beat the egg whites in a bowl until stiff peaks form. Fold into the custard. Chill for at least 1 hour.

For the topping, place a glass or stainless steel bowl in the freezer for 10 to 15 minutes. Pour the cream into the bowl. Beat at high speed until frothy. Add the sugar and vanilla gradually. Beat on high speed until firm peaks form.

Spoon the custard into serving bowls. Top with the topping. Sprinkle with nutmeg to serve.

Makes 6 to 8 servings

Cathy Wood-Rupert

Tip: To scald milk, heat to 180 degrees, stirring constantly. The milk should just begin to come to a light froth, with tiny bubbles forming around the edge of the pan.

New Orleans Bread Pudding with Whiskey Sauce

Pudding
1 loaf dry French bread
2 cups milk or heavy cream
2 eggs, beaten
1 cup sugar
1/2 cup (1 stick) butter, softened
1 teaspoon vanilla extract
1 cup pecans, chopped

Whiskey Sauce
3/4 cup sugar
1 egg
1/2 cup (1 stick) butter, melted
1/4 cup bourbon

For the pudding, tear the bread into pieces. Combine with the milk in a large bowl and let stand until all the liquid is absorbed. Add the eggs, sugar, butter, vanilla and pecans and mix well.

Butter the bottom and sides of an 8×10-inch baking dish very generously. Pour the bread mixture into the dish. Bake at 350 degrees for about 45 minutes or until a knife inserted into the center comes out clean. The pudding should be firm and light golden brown.

For the sauce, beat the sugar and egg in a bowl until creamy. Add the butter. Stir until the sugar dissolves. Stir in the bourbon.

Cut the pudding into squares. Pour the sauce over the top and serve.

Makes 8 servings

Lesley Miller

CARROT CAKE

1 pound baby carrots, shredded
4 eggs
1 cup vegetable oil
2 cups sugar
1 teaspoon baking soda
1 teaspoon baking powder
1 teaspoon salt
2 teaspoons cinnamon
2 cups all-purpose flour
Cream Cheese Frosting (page 201)

Combine the carrots, eggs, oil, sugar, baking soda, baking powder, salt and cinnamon in a large bowl and mix well. Add the flour 1 cup at a time, mixing after each addition until well combined.

Pour the batter into a greased 9×13-inch baking pan or two 9-inch baking pans. Bake at 325 degrees for 50 to 60 minutes for a 9×13-inch cake or 35 to 45 minutes for 9-inch cakes or until a wooden pick inserted in the center comes out clean. Let cool completely; remove from the pan to a serving platter. Frost the top and sides with Cream Cheese Frosting.

Makes 1 cake

Susan Landry

CHOCOLATE CUPCAKES

2 cups sugar
1 3/4 cups all-purpose flour
3/4 cup baking cocoa
2 teaspoons baking soda
1 teaspoon baking powder
1 teaspoon salt
2 eggs
1 cup strong brewed coffee
1 cup buttermilk
1/2 cup vegetable oil
1 teaspoon vanilla extract

Combine the sugar, flour, baking cocoa, baking soda, baking powder and salt in a large mixing bowl. Add the eggs, coffee, buttermilk, oil and vanilla and mix well. Spoon the batter into paper-lined muffin cups. Bake at 350 degrees for 45 to 50 minutes until a wooden pick inserted in the center comes out clean.

Makes 12 cupcakes

Susan Landry

Tip: *This versatile batter can also be baked in a bundt pan then dusted with confectioners' sugar, or baked as a sheet cake or in layers. It's excellent topped with Vanilla or Chocolate Buttercream Frosting, or with Cream Cheese or Peanut Butter Frosting (pages 200–201).*

LEMON CAKE

CAKE
1 (18-ounce) package white cake mix
1 (3-ounce) package lemon gelatin mix
3/4 cup vegetable oil
3/4 cup water
4 eggs

LEMON GLAZE
2 cups confectioners' sugar, sifted
1/2 cup (1 stick) butter, melted
1/2 cup fresh lemon juice

For the cake, combine the cake mix, gelatin mix, oil and water in a large bowl and mix well. Beat in the eggs one at a time, mixing after each addition until well blended. Pour into a generously greased 9×13-inch baking dish. Bake at 350 degrees for 35 to 40 minutes until firm in the center and golden brown.

For the glaze, combine the confectioners' sugar, butter and lemon juice and mix well. Poke holes in the cake with a fork. Pour the glaze over the cake.

Makes 10 servings

Jeff Miller

Tip: *To be sure your cake won't stick to the pan, dust a greased cake pan with 1 tablespoon plain bread crumbs, which have a more pleasant taste than flour residue.*

TRES LECHES CAKE

CAKE
1 1/3 cups all-purpose flour
1 teaspoon baking powder
1/2 teaspoon salt
1/2 cup (1 stick) butter, softened
1 cup sugar
5 eggs
1 1/2 teaspoons vanilla extract

LECHE MIXTURE
1 (12-ounce) can evaporated milk
1 (14-ounce) can sweetened condensed milk
1 cup half-and-half
Whipped cream

For the cake, sift together the flour, baking powder and salt. Beat the butter in a bowl with an electric mixer until creamy. Add the sugar and beat until blended. Add the eggs one at a time. Add the vanilla and mix well. Add the flour mixture one-third at a time, mixing just until combined after each addition. Pour the batter into a greased 9×13-inch baking pan. Bake at 350 degrees for 20 to 25 minutes until a wooden pick inserted in the center comes out clean.

For the leche mixture, combine the evaporated milk, condensed milk and half-and-half in a bowl and mix well. Use a fork to poke holes in the top of the cake. Pour the milk mixture over the cake. Chill for at least 8 hours. Top with whipped cream to serve.

Makes 8 servings

Rodrigo Neder

Vanilla Buttercream Frosting

3/4 cup (1 1/2 sticks) butter, softened
5 to 6 cups confectioners' sugar
6 to 7 teaspoons cream or milk
2 teaspoons vanilla extract
Pinch of salt

Beat the butter in a bowl with an electric mixer until creamy. Beat in 2 cups of the confectioners' sugar gradually until well blended. Add the remaining confectioners' sugar and cream alternately, beating until well blended. Beat for 2 minutes longer. Add the vanilla and salt. Beat for 1 minute.

Makes enough frosting for 1 cake or 24 cupcakes

Susan Landry

Peanut Butter Frosting

6 tablespoons butter, softened
6 tablespoons creamy peanut butter
5 to 6 cups confectioners' sugar
6 to 7 tablespoons cream or milk

Beat the butter and peanut butter in a bowl with an electric mixer until well blended. Beat in 2 cups of the confectioners' sugar gradually. Add the remaining confectioners' sugar and cream alternately, beating until well blended. Beat for 2 minutes longer. Add the vanilla and salt. Beat for 1 minute.

Makes enough frosting for 1 cake or 24 cupcakes

Susan Landry

Chocolate Buttercream Frosting

$1/2$ cup (1 stick) butter, melted
$2/3$ cup baking cocoa
3 cups confectioners' sugar
$1/3$ cup milk
1 teaspoon vanilla extract

Beat the butter and baking cocoa in a bowl with an electric mixer until well blended. Add the confectioners' sugar and milk alternately, beating at medium speed after each addition until well blended. Add the vanilla. Beat for 1 minute longer.

Makes enough frosting for 1 cake or 24 cupcakes

Susan Landry

Cream Cheese Frosting

5 tablespoons butter, softened
8 ounces cream cheese, softened
3 cups confectioners' sugar
2 teaspoons vanilla extract

Beat the butter and cream cheese in a bowl with an electric mixer until well blended. Add the confectioners' sugar 1 cup at a time, beating after each addition until creamy and well blended. Add the vanilla. Beat for 1 minute longer.

Makes enough frosting for 1 cake or 24 cupcakes

Susan Landry

ALMOND BISCOTTI

1 1/2 cups all-purpose flour, sifted
1 1/2 teaspoons baking powder
1/4 teaspoon salt
1/2 cup yellow cornmeal
1/2 cup (1 stick) unsalted butter, softened
1 cup sugar
2 eggs
1 teaspoon almond extract
3/4 cup sliced almonds

Combine the flour, baking powder, salt and cornmeal in a bowl and mix well. Beat the butter and sugar in a bowl with an electric mixer for 2 minutes. Add the eggs and extract and mix well. Add the dry ingredients and beat until well combined. Stir in the almonds by hand.

Divide the dough into two equal parts. Roll each part into a 12-inch-long log. Press the dough until it is about 4 inches wide.

Place the flattened logs on a baking parchment-lined baking sheet. Bake at 350 degrees until springy and golden brown. Remove from the oven and turn off the oven.

Cut the flattened logs on the diagonal into 1-inch-wide slices. Arrange on the baking sheet. Return to the warm oven. Let bake for 10 minutes until golden brown and crisp.

Makes 24 cookies

Danielle Gephardt, Papa Leone's

Tip: *The second baking process for biscotti is done in an oven that is cooling down throughout the baking process. This allows the biscotti to become crisp without becoming hard.*

BUTTER PECAN COOKIES

1 cup (2 sticks) unsalted
butter, softened
1 cup sugar

1 egg
2 cups all-purpose flour
2 cups pecan halves

Beat the butter and sugar in a bowl with an electric mixer until creamy. Add the egg and mix well. Beat in the flour at low speed until well blended. Stir in the pecans by hand.

Scoop out the dough by teaspoonfuls, making sure there are at least two pecan halves per teaspoon. Space the dough portions 3 inches apart on a baking parchment-lined baking sheet. Bake at 350 degrees for 13 to 14 minutes. Let cool completely on the baking sheet.

Makes 60 cookies

Marlene Meyer

FRENCH BUTTERCREAM COOKIES

1 1/2 cups confectioners'
sugar, sifted
1 teaspoon cream of tartar
1/4 teaspoon salt

1 cup (2 sticks) butter, softened
1 egg
1 teaspoon vanilla extract
2 1/4 cups all-purpose flour

Combine the confectioners' sugar, cream of tartar and salt in a bowl and mix well. Add the butter, egg and vanilla and mix well. Add the flour gradually. Chill the dough for 1 hour.

Shape the dough into nickel-size balls. Arrange on a baking parchment-lined baking sheet. Use a fork to flatten and score the cookies. Bake at 350 degrees for 5 to 8 minutes until light brown. Let cool on the baking sheet for 1 minute. Remove to a cooling rack to cool completely.

Makes 48 cookies

Susan Landry

OATMEAL CHOCOLATE CHIP COOKIES

1¹/2 cups all-purpose flour
1 teaspoon salt
1 teaspoon baking soda
¹/2 cup shortening
¹/2 cup (1 stick) butter, softened
1 cup brown sugar
¹/2 cup granulated sugar
2 eggs
2 tablespoons water
1 teaspoon vanilla extract
3 cups rolled oats
1 cup chocolate chips or raisins
¹/2 cup wheat germ
1 cup walnuts, chopped (optional)

Sift together the flour, salt and baking soda. Combine the shortening, butter and brown sugar in a bowl. Beat until creamy. Add the granulated sugar, eggs, water and vanilla and mix well. Add the flour mixture and mix well. Stir in the oats, chocolate chips, wheat germ and walnuts.

Drop teaspoonfuls of the dough onto an ungreased cookie sheet. Bake at 350 degrees for 12 to 15 minutes until golden brown.

Makes 56 cookies

Mary Lou Mullen

SUGAR COOKIES

2¹/2 cups all-purpose flour, sifted
¹/2 teaspoon baking powder
¹/4 teaspoon salt
¹/2 cup (1 stick) butter, softened
¹/2 cup shortening

1 cup sugar
1 egg
1 teaspoon vanilla extract
2 tablespoons skim milk
Additional sugar

Sift together the flour, baking powder and salt. Beat the butter and shortening in a bowl with an electric mixer until creamy. Add the sugar and beat until fluffy. Beat in the egg and vanilla. Add the flour mixture and mix well. Add the milk and mix well.

Drop teaspoonfuls of dough onto a greased cookie sheet. Flatten each cookie with the flat bottom of a glass that has been greased and dipped in additional sugar.

Bake at 400 degrees for 12 minutes until the edges are light brown. Cool on a wire rack.

Makes 72 cookies

Kay Wohlson

CHOCOLATE RASPBERRY BARS

2 cups all-purpose flour
¹/2 cup brown sugar
1 cup (2 sticks) butter, softened
1³/4 cups chocolate chips

1 (14-ounce) can sweetened
   condensed milk
1 cup seedless raspberry jam

Combine the flour, brown sugar and butter in a bowl and mix well. Press half over the bottom of a 9×13-inch baking pan. Bake at 350 degrees for 10 minutes. Maintain the oven temperature.

Reserve a handful of the chocolate chips. Combine the remaining chocolate chips and the condensed milk in a medium saucepan. Cook until the chocolate chips are melted. Pour over the hot baked layer. Top with the remaining flour mixture. Drop spoonfuls of jam over the top. Sprinkle with the reserved chocolate chips. Bake for 40 minutes. Cool completely. Cut into 24 bars.

Makes 24 bars

Susan Landry

FRUITCAKE COOKIES

Even if you've never been a fan of fruitcake, these cookies are absolutely worth trying. They make an excellent holiday cookie for parties and gift giving.

2 cups (about) all-purpose flour for dredging
2 pounds red and green candied cherries
2 pounds red and green candied pineapple
6 cups pecans, chopped
1/2 cup (1 stick) butter
1 1/2 cups dark brown sugar
1 cup granulated sugar

4 eggs
3 cups all-purpose flour for the cookies
1 tablespoon baking soda
1 teaspoon salt
1 teaspoon cinnamon
1 teaspoon allspice
1 teaspoon ground cloves
3 tablespoons milk
1 cup whiskey

Pour 1/2 cup of the dredging flour into a large bowl. Add 1 pound of the candied fruit. Toss the pieces to coat with flour. Cut the fruit into small pieces, dusting with additional dredging flour often to prevent the knife and fruit from becoming sticky. Flour and chop the remaining fruit in the same manner. Add the pecans to the fruit and mix.

Beat the butter with the brown sugar, granulated sugar and eggs in a bowl. Combine 3 cups flour, the baking soda, salt, cinnamon, allspice and cloves in a bowl. Combine the butter mixture and the dry ingredients gradually until well combined. Add the milk and whiskey and mix well. Fold the fruit mixture into the batter with a heavy wooden spoon; the batter will become very heavy when all the fruit is added.

Drop heaping teaspoonfuls of the dough onto greased baking sheets. Bake at 350 degrees for 11 minutes.

Makes 13 dozen cookies

Betty Higman

Tip: You may substitute candied citron, raisins, or dates for the candied pineapple and cherries.

KOURAMBIETHES
(POWDERED SHORTBREAD COOKIES)

These lovely Greek shortbread cookies are traditionally baked
during the Easter season and can be modified in many ways. Use a citrus
zest or extract, add nuts, or change the liquor or perhaps top with a glaze.
Whatever you add, what you must do is try them.

1 cup (2 sticks) unsalted butter, softened
1 cup confectioners' sugar
1 egg yolk
3 tablespoons brandy or whiskey
3/4 teaspoon vanilla extract
2 1/4 cups (about) all-purpose flour
1/2 teaspoon baking powder
1/2 cup blanched almonds, finely chopped (optional)
1/2 cup confectioners' sugar

Beat the butter in a large bowl with an electric mixer for 10 minutes until light and fluffy. Add 1 cup of the confectioners' sugar gradually and beat for another 10 minutes until the mixture is very pale. Combine the egg yolk, brandy and vanilla in a small bowl. Add to the butter mixture.

Combine half the flour with the baking powder. Add to the butter mixture and mix well. Add the remaining flour and mix to form a soft, smooth dough that is easy to work with. (The dough will become stiff if too much flour is added.) Add the almonds.

Flatten walnut-size pieces of dough and form them into a crescent, or cut into other shapes using a cookie cutter. Bake on an ungreased baking sheet at 350 degrees for 15 to 20 minutes until cookies are pale yellow. Cool on a rack. Sprinkle generously with 1/2 cup confectioners' sugar.

Makes 48 cookies

Anna Epislantis

APPLE PRALINE PIE

FILLING
5 cups diced peeled apples
3/4 cup sugar
1/4 cup all-purpose flour
1 teaspoon cinnamon
1/4 teaspoon salt

TOPPING
1/4 cup (1/2 stick) butter
1/2 cup packed brown sugar
2 tablespoons milk
1/2 cup pecans, chopped

PASTRY AND ASSEMBLY
1 recipe Pie Pastry (page 211), or 2 refrigerator pie pastries
2 tablespoons butter, chilled and cut into small pieces

For the filling, combine the apples, sugar, flour, cinnamon and salt in a bowl. Toss to coat the apples.

For the topping, combine the butter, brown sugar and milk in a saucepan. Bring to a boil. Remove from the heat. Stir in the pecans.

To assemble, fit one of the pastries into a 9-inch pie plate. Spoon the filling into the pastry. Dot with the butter. Top with the second pastry, sealing and fluting the edge. Cut several slits in the top pastry for steam to escape.

Spread the topping over the top. Place the pie plate on a baking sheet. Bake at 425 degrees for 35 to 45 minutes, covering the edge with foil after 15 minutes to prevent overbrowning. The pie is done when the crust is golden brown, the topping is bubbling and the apples are tender.

Makes 8 servings

Julie Ann Coyne

Fruit Tart

Pastry

1 cup all-purpose flour
6 tablespoons butter, cut into
1-tablespoon pieces and frozen
2 tablespoons sugar
1 egg yolk
1 tablespoon cold water
1/8 teaspoon salt

Filling

4 eggs, beaten
3/4 cup sugar
1/4 cup (1/2 stick) butter
1/4 cup heavy cream
1/2 cup lemon juice
3 tablespoons orange juice

Assembly

1 pint berries, any type or
a mixture

For the pastry, combine the flour, butter, sugar, egg yolk, water and salt in a food processor. Pulse several times for a total of 5 seconds. Continue until the dough forms a ball. Wrap in waxed paper. Refrigerate until ready to use.

For the filling, combine the eggs, sugar, butter, cream, lemon juice and orange juice in a saucepan. Cook over medium heat for about 10 minutes or until the mixture is thick and well blended, stirring constantly.

Roll the pastry dough on a floured surface. Fit into a 9-inch pie plate. Bake at 350 degrees for 15 minutes or until the edge is light brown. Fill with the filling. Bake for 20 minutes until the filling is set. Let cool completely. Top with the berries. Serve the tart the day it is baked.

Makes 6 to 8 servings

Anne West

Tip: For ease in "blind baking" the crust, use a coffee filter the size of the pie dish and fill with whatever weights you are using (beans, pie weights, etc). When the crust is done baking, you can simply remove the filter.

LEMON MERINGUE PIE

1/2 recipe Pie Pastry (page 211)

FILLING
1 cup plus 1 tablespoon sugar
1/2 cup all-purpose flour
1/4 teaspoon salt
1 tablespoon lemon zest
1/2 cup lemon juice
3 cups milk

5 egg yolks, lightly beaten
3 tablespoons butter
2 teaspoons vanilla extract

MERINGUE
5 egg whites, at room temperature
1/2 teaspoon vanilla extract
1/2 teaspoon cream of tartar
1/2 cup sugar (preferably superfine)

Fit the pastry into a 9- or 10-inch pie plate. Bake at 425 degrees for 12 to 15 minutes until golden brown.

For the filling, combine the sugar, flour and salt in a heavy saucepan. Add the lemon zest and lemon juice. Add the milk gradually. Cook over medium heat, stirring constantly.

Add a small amount of the hot lemon mixture to the yolks to temper them. Stir the yolks into the hot lemon mixture. Cook for 5 minutes or until the spoon leaves an indentation in the mixture, stirring constantly. Remove from the heat. Stir in the butter and vanilla. Pour into the pastry shell.

For the meringue, beat the egg whites in a bowl with an electric mixer until soft peaks form. Add the vanilla and cream of tartar. Add the sugar gradually, beating until stiff peaks form and the sugar is dissolved. Spread the meringue over the hot filling, sealing to the edge. Bake at 350 degrees for 12 to 15 minutes until meringue is golden brown.

Makes 8 servings

Betty Higman

Tip: Adding a small amount of the hot mixture to the egg yolks is called "tempering." This is done to avoid cooking the egg yolks when they are added to the hot mixture.

Lemon Meringue Pie Variations

Chocolate Pie

Increase the sugar in the filling to 1^1/3 cups and omit the lemon zest and lemon juice. Add 2 ounces chopped unsweetened chocolate when adding the milk.

Butterscotch Pie

Omit the lemon zest and lemon juice from the filling. Substitute dark brown sugar for the granulated sugar in the filling.

Banana Cream Pie

Omit the lemon zest and lemon juice from the filling. Slice 3 bananas into the baked pie shell. Top with the filling and meringue.

Coconut Cream Pie

Omit the lemon zest and juice from the filling, and add 2 cups flaked coconut. Top the baked meringue with 1/3 cup toasted coconut.

Pie Pastry

2 cups all-purpose flour	3/4 cup shortening
1 teaspoon sugar	1 teaspoon vinegar
1/2 teaspoon salt	5 tablespoons ice water

Sift the flour, sugar and salt into a mixing bowl. Cut in the shortening with a fork or pastry blender until the mixture resembles coarse cornmeal. Combine the water and vinegar in a small bowl. Sprinkle over the flour mixture 1 tablespoon at a time. Toss lightly with a fork, pushing the dampened dough to the side of the bowl. The dough should be just moist enough to hold together. Refrigerate for 1 hour before rolling pastry thinly on a lightly floured board.

If using this crust for a cream-filled pie, fit the pastry into a pie plate. Bake at 425 degrees for 12 to 15 minutes.

Makes enough pastry for 2 crusts or 4 individual tarts

Betty Higman

CHERRY PIE

3 tablespoons cornstarch
1/4 cup water
1 (14-ounce) can tart red cherries, juice reserved
1 cup frozen dark sweet cherries
3/4 cup sugar
1 teaspoon lemon juice
1 recipe Pie Pastry (page 211)

Combine the cornstarch and water in a small bowl and mix well. Pour the reserved cherry juice into a saucepan. Bring to a boil over low heat. As soon as the juice begins to boil, stir in the sugar and cornstarch mixture. Add the cherries, stirring constantly. The filling will thicken quickly. Remove from the heat. Add the lemon juice.

Let cool slightly. Line 4 individual tart pans with the pastry. Pour the filling evenly into each pastry shell. Top each with a lattice crust. Bake at 350 degrees for 30 minutes or until the crust is brown.

Makes 4 individual pies

Tip: For a decorative topping on any fruit pie, cut the lattice strips with a crimped pastry wheel for a lacy look. Brush the strips with an egg wash before topping the pie.

PUMPKIN PIE

3 eggs, beaten
1 (15-ounce) can pumpkin
(not pumpkin pie filling)
3/4 cup sugar
1/2 teaspoon salt
1 teaspoon cinnamon
1/4 teaspoon freshly grated nutmeg
1 1/2 cups half-and-half
1 tablespoon all-purpose flour
1 teaspoon vanilla extract
1/2 recipe Pie Pastry (page 211)

Combine the eggs, pumpkin, sugar, salt, cinnamon, nutmeg, half-and-half, flour and vanilla in a large bowl and mix well.

Fit the pastry into a 9-inch pie plate. Pour the pumpkin filling into the shell. Bake at 400 degrees for 15 minutes. Decrease the oven temperature to 350 degrees. Bake for 40 to 50 minutes longer until a knife inserted in the center comes out clean. Serve with sweetened whipped cream or ice cream.

Makes 8 servings

Deanna Urner

Tip: A perfect topping for pumpkin pie is homemade whipped cream. For the best results, always chill the bowl, beaters, and heavy whipping cream before starting.

SWEET POTATO PIE

1/2 cup (1 stick) butter
1/2 cup miniature marshmallows
2 cups mashed cooked sweet potatoes
1 1/2 cups granulated sugar
1 teaspoon cinnamon
1 teaspoon nutmeg
1/2 cup brown sugar
3 large eggs, beaten
1 (12-ounce) can evaporated milk
1 recipe Pie Pastry (page 211)

Melt the butter and marshmallows in a saucepan over low heat, stirring until smooth and well blended. Remove from the heat. Add the sweet potatoes and mix well.

Combine the granulated sugar, cinnamon and nutmeg. Add to the sweet potato mixture. Add the brown sugar, eggs and evaporated milk and mix well.

Fit the pastries into two 9-inch pie plates. Divide the sweet potato mixture equally between the shells. Bake at 400 degrees for 10 minutes. Reduce the oven temperature to 350 degrees and bake 40 to 50 minutes longer. Cover the edges with aluminum foil if they begin to brown too quickly.

Makes 2 pies

Donna Rich

Tip: Oven temperatures can vary, so get to know your oven. Test with an oven thermometer to be sure that the temperature is accurate. If you are baking a new recipe, you may want to check it a few times to be sure that the baking process is going according to the directions.

Chef Manolo Acin of
  The Harbor Court Hotel, Baltimore
Karen Adkins
Susan Bridges
Julie Ann Coyne
Connie Crabtree-Burritt
Bruce Dorsey of
  The Metropolitan Cafe
Anna Epislantis
Aaron Fries
A.J. Furay
Danielle Gephardt of Papa Leone's
Pat Goodyear
Mary Graul
Chef Edwin "Zeus" Harmon of
  The Harbor Court Hotel, Baltimore
Barbara Hettleman
Betty Higman
Pat Himmelrich
Bruce Kirby
Susan Landry
Beth Lebow
Hans Mayer
Marlene Meyer
Jeff Miller
Lesley Miller

Alan Morestein of Regi's
Cassie Motz
Mary Lou Mullen
Rodrigo Neder
Katie O'Malley, First Lady of Maryland
Anne Puckett
Donna Rich
Betty Robinson
Chef Ronald Robinson of
  The Harbor Court Hotel, Baltimore
Executive Chef Josean Rosado of
  The Harbor Court Hotel, Baltimore
Jane Sabatelli
John Sabatelli
Gail Shawe
Frieda Ullman
Deanna Urner
Bill Van Dyke
Julia Van Dyke
Belinda Waterman
Sylvia Weaver
Berry Werner of
  Scarborough Fair Bed & Breakfast
Anne West
Kay Wohlson
Cathy Wood-Rupert